THE WORLD BOOK OF

Soups

The World Book of Soups

NINA FROUD

DRAKE PUBLISHERS INC
NEW YORK

Published in 1972 by
Drake Publishers Inc
381 Park Avenue South
New York, N.Y. 10016

ISBN 87749-225-5

Printed in Great Britain

For

H. U.

because he likes

my soups

CONTENTS

ACKNOWLEDGEMENTS

I should like to thank the following for their kindness and generosity in contributing recipes for this book: Mrs Eva Alfert for her Jewish recipes; Avenida Palace Hotel, Barcelona for Hazelnut soup; Senora Marina Pereira de Aznar for Canary Islands soups; Nicholas Kaye Ltd and Mrs Elizabeth Gill for Mimosa and Costa Brava soups from her mother-in-law's excellent collection *Tia Victoria's Spanish Kitchen;* to Faber and Faber for permission to reproduce my own recipe of Andalusian Gazpacho from the *Home Book of Spanish Cookery;* to Grete Grumme for Danish Buttermilk and Elderberry soup recipes; to chef Vittorio Zanda for his Italian Wedding soup; Madame Georgette Viala of the Mon Plaisir Restaurant in London, for her bisque; The Golden Dragon Restaurant and the management of The Mandarin Hotel in Hong Kong for Sharks' Fin and Birds' Nest soups respectively; to Gallery Rendezvous Chinese Restaurant in London for Hot and Sour soup; to La Confrèrie Nationale Brillat-Savarine de Taste Fromage for their cheese soup recipes; Mrs Louise Geis, Mrs D. Loewenthal and Mrs Pearl Lee for Israeli recipes; Dr Aya Kagawa for her help with Japanese recipes; Signora Albina Dell'Omo for her Italian fish soup; June O'Brien for American and Canadian specialities; the chefs of the Ararat and Aragvi Restaurants in Moscow for their recipes of soups from the Caucasus; the management of the Viking Hotel in Oslo for Norwegian Chervil soup; the Cockpit Hotel in Singapore for Indonesian and Malaysian recipes; to Moti Mahai Restaurant, New Delhi, for Indian recipes; and last, but most important of all, I wish to acknowledge my debt to my late father-in-law, George Froud, from whom I learnt so much about Russian soups and their splendid accompaniments. I should also like to express my gratitude to Miss Kathleen Tranmar for all her good work in making the manuscript presentable.

N.F.

'Soo—oop of the e—e—evening,
Beautiful, beauti—FUL SOUP!'
(Lewis Carroll, *Alice's Adventures in Wonderland*)

Je vis de bonne soupe et non de beau langage.
(Moliere, *Les Femmes Savantes*)

Tutto fa brodo.
(Italian proverb)

A broth of a boy.
(Irish expression)

INTRODUCTION

I am unashamedly addicted to good soups. Nothing can rival a fine soup as a prelude to a meal. Many soups make a splendid and satisfying meal.

For too many years now, ever since the manufacturers of the meat extracts and soup concentrates began flooding the markets with their wares, efforts have gone on to brainwash us into thinking that the era of the stock pot and the home-made soup is gone. Don't you believe it! How can anyone presume to tell us that, by dropping a cube of some compressed chemical extract into a pan of water, we can, in a matter of minutes, produce broth 'like grandmother used to make'? People who would swallow that, would swallow anything, including substandard soups.

There is no need for us to go to the trouble our grandmothers' procedures involved. Many good soups are quick and easy to make. Once you have eaten and served soups made of vegetables which you brought home *fresh,* with a little cream and butter stirred in at the last moment and seasoned to *your* liking, you will never again use tins or packets of soups, for pleasure. Your taste buds won't let you. The better stock cubes are fine in emergencies, but they should be used with caution. Often an attempt to concentrate the flavour results in unpalatable over-salting. They are better than plain water, but they are no substitute for a real base for a good, nourishing delicious broth.

In many Eastern countries, where the cooking facilities which we in the West take for granted are totally absent, there never has been any such thing as a stock pot permanently on the simmer. How could there have been when all a woman may have in the way of a kitchen is half a dozen bricks which serve her as a charcoal brazier? Yet it doesn't stop her producing exceedingly good soups, without the help of concentrates. Refrigerators, too, are not easy to come by, especially in the country, so stock has to be made fresh every day. Oriental cooks hasten the process by cutting all ingredients into small pieces.

Soups have a long history. Some of the Middle East soups still retain a biblical flavour.

In the West, in countries with a tradition for good eating, soup has always been the first item on the menu. The Greeks, who had a word for everything, have one for a super fish soup, which has spread to other Mediterranean countries, to become bouillabaisse in France and bullabesa in Spain. Their celebrated avgolemono soup is often based on fish stock. The recipe for this is in the section for Special Soups, which refuse to fit under convenient headings. In France, the Pot-au-feu is not only a magnificent dish in its own right and the basis for most meat soups, but an institution, a symbol of a well-regulated family.

For country people, in most parts of the world, soup constitutes an entire meal. In Russia the soups have long been a staple diet and a popular saying is 'shchi da kasha – pishcha nasha', which means: 'shchi and kasha is our mainstay'. Perhaps necessity has done something towards begetting invention. The Russians have certainly developed a tradition of excellent soups with mouth-watering accompaniments of coulibiacs and pirozhki, substantial enough to make a complete meal.

The danger of such Russian soups is that one wants more than one helping and it would need a very robust appetite to take them into one's stride merely as a first course.

At home, when my late father-in-law did the cooking, we made it a rule that his superlative soups with blinchiki or pirog were served as a main course.

He was an extraordinary old gentleman: the only Englishman to have served in the battleship Potemkin during the Russo-Japanese war; the only Englishman, to my knowledge, who felt 'Russian' enough to drive a taxi in Paris; and the only Englishman who could present Russian soups and coulibiacs in all their glory.

The Italians, with their genius for pasta products, have a great variety of pasta in brodo. The importance of soups in the Italian scheme of things can be gleaned from the name of their most famous soup – minestrone, which has its origins in an old verb which means to serve food, to minister to the needs of the hungry. They also have a range of great fish soups and I have read in an Italian journal the ungallant guess that the reason for Lord Byron's prolonged stay in Italy was not due to his romantic involvements but to his inability to resist Adriatic fish soups.

In the Scandinavian countries some soups, such as the Thursday split pea soup, are regular weekly features on family menus, the way a roast joint is supposed to be a must on Sundays in Britain.

There are many such meal-in-themselves soups in many countries; the French Pot-au-feu, the Polish Krupnik, Russian Borsch and Shchi, Argentine Puchero, Bolivian Chupe, Scotch Broth, Spanish Cocido, Galician Pote, Siberian Pelmeni, Chinese Ta Pin Lo – marvellous for cold evenings, Brazilian Chicken and Rice soup, Cock-a-leekie, Flemish Waterzootje, Chinese Chicken Chowder, Florida Seafood Bisque, Caribbean Crab Gumbo, Breton Cotriade and most other fish soups – bouillabaisse, certainly ukha, if served with its correct accompaniments, and others.

It is interesting to note how many of the fruit soups have evolved in northern countries. The valuable juices of bottled fruit and berries compensate for the absence of fresh produce during the winter months. Fruit soups are served hot in the winter. In the summer, when there is an abundance of berries of all kinds, they are served cold.

Many of these fruit soups could easily be served as desserts. After all, where does one draw a line between a fruit cocktail and a fruit salad?

Many of the vegetable soups can be made totally vegetarian by using water instead of stock.

In the East, soups form an essential part of the menu, whether the meal is a banquet in an elegant restaurant or a modest home meal, though soups are not necessarily served as a first course. Chinese soups, for instance, the variety and subtlety of which is endless, are generally speaking, clear and light and, therefore, often served between courses or at the end of the meal, to freshen the palate.

A dozen ingredients is a fair average for a good Ta Pin Lo, though there can be more. There is a recipe for a popular sap kam ('Ten Item Pot'), which includes chicken, wun tun, noodles, Chinese smoked ham, fried bean curd, sliced fish quenelles and trepang or abalone.

Malaysian cooks often use coconut milk (p. 151) for soups instead of stock. If you live in the right place, coconuts can be had for nothing. Meat never is.

The best known Korean specialities are 'kooks', soups often of such thick consistency that they qualify as stews. The Koreans like their soups piping hot, though they have a proverb which says: 'One can't taste the flavour of boiling soup.' To make their soups even more nourishing, Korean housewives use a garnish of wafer-thin omelette rolled and cut into shreds.

In Burma a soup is a must on any menu and is invariably clear, usually based on fish stock, frequently garnished with fresh or dried prawns and flavoured with nga-pi-yet, fish sauce which most Europeans find too pungent. Pounded anchovy fillet makes a good substitute. To make a light stock, the Burmese cook allows a large Pacific prawn and a ¼ litre (half pint or one cup) water per portion. The prawns are brought to a boil with a crushed garlic, a chopped onion and a teaspoon of balachaung – dried prawns pounded to a paste with spices (p. 150). To turn this into a soup, shredded vegetables are added and simmered until just done. The soup is often served with boiled rice and used as a gravy.

Mulligatawny is the best known of Indian soups. So much so that it is often thought of as an English speciality! In fact, it is not just one soup, there are many kinds – all mulligatawnies. The name means 'pepper water' and this soup originated as a cure for indigestion. In India pepper water is served with dry curries. It can be based on meat, chicken, fish or vegetable stock. For plain pepper water, the spices are fried in a little ghee with chopped onion, garlic and dry chillis, using water acidulated with tamarind juice (p. 157) as stock.

Japan has a wide variety of clear and thick soups. All soups are based on dashi (p. 21) and the Japanese housewife is greatly concerned with the visual appeal of her soups. The utensil in which it is served gets as much attention as the garnish which goes into it. Clear soups, called suimono, are distinguished by decorative simplicity. The main accent is on freshness of raw materials and a careful balance between preserving their natural flavour and judiciously enhancing them by various processes. The thick soups called sumashi-shiru or miso-shiru, are thickened with miso, fermented bean paste. Miso is clean and pleasant to taste, is a valuable source of vitamins and keeps indefinitely.

Among the Japanese soup recipes included in this book, are chawan mushi, a delicious custard soup, and Zoni. To make zoni, tradition says, only wakamizu, 'young water', drawn at break of dawn on New Year's day, is good enough and it is 'lucky' to serve zoni at New Year Festival.

This superstition connected with soups crops up in many countries. In Sweden, the split pea soup is said to bring luck if served at New Year. (It also uses up the ham bones left over from Christmas.) In China a noodle soup plays a special part at birthday dinners, for noodles symbolise long life. When serving noodles, they must never be cut or broken off in any way, as that 'shortens the life'.

I hope the collection of recipes in this book illustrates the versatility of soups. There are fabulously luxurious and extravagant

Russian soups, such as Madame Molokhovets' Salmon and Champagne Ukha (especially if clarified with caviar) and frugally economical soups, such as Austrian Caraway Soup (especially if cooked with monastic simplicity in water instead of stock).

There are delicate consommés and hearty peasant broths, subtle Oriental soups, creamy purée soups, soups to warm and comfort on a freezing day and chilled soups to refresh and stimulate the appetite during a heat wave.

ABBREVIATIONS

oz	–	ounce
lb	–	pound
gr	–	gram
kg	–	kilogram
ml	–	millilitre
dcl	–	decilitre

MEASUREMENTS

The ingredients are given in Continental, English and American weights and measures. These are not always straight conversions from the English measures, but suitable adjustments. Where, for the sake of convenience, 1 oz is shown as 30 grams, instead of 28.35, amounts of all ingredients have been proportionally scaled up or down. The cups, tablespoons and teaspoons are American standard.

OVEN TEMPERATURES

Oven temperatures are given in all recipes in °C, °F and Gas Regulo. Allowances, however, have to be made for variations of settings on different models of electric cookers and it is advisable to consult the instructions supplied with the cookers.

Basic Preparations

BEEF STOCK (BROWN STOCK)

- 2 kg (4 lb) soup bones
- 2 kg (4 lb) veal knuckle
- $1\frac{1}{2}$ kg (3 lb) shin beef, or other cheap cut
- 60 grs (2 oz or 4 tablespoons) butter
- 2 large chopped onions
- 2–3 medium-sized chopped carrots
- $2\frac{1}{2}$ litre (5 pints or 10 cups) cold water
- 250 grs (8 oz) piece fresh pork skin
- bouquet garni
- $1\frac{1}{2}$ tablespoons salt

Have the bones and the knuckle sawn into pieces. Cut the meat into large cubes.

In the stock pot heat butter and lightly fry the vegetables. Add bones, knuckle and beef and brown.

Add $\frac{1}{2}$ litre (1 pint or 2 cups) water, bring to the boil, add pork skin, reduce heat and simmer very slowly until the water almost boils away. Add remaining water, bouquet garni and salt. Simmer gently for several hours. Strain, cool, remove surface fat. If necessary, clarify as described in recipe for consommé (p. 85) and use as required.

VEAL STOCK (WHITE STOCK)

- 1 kg (2 lb) shoulder of veal
- 1 kg (2 lb) veal knuckle
- chicken carcass or giblets (optional)
- 4 litres (4 quarts) cold water
- 2 large sliced onions
- 2 medium-sized quartered
- 1 shredded stalk celery carrots
- 2 sliced leeks
- bouquet garni
- salt

Have the butcher bone the meat and saw or chop the bones. Put the bones in a stock pot, add water and bring to the boil. If you have any chicken bones or giblets, add them to the pot. Remove surface scum, add onion, carrots, leeks, celery and bouquet garni. Cover and simmer slowly for 4–5 hours. Season and taste the stock for flavour. If it is not strong enough, remove lid and boil down to reduce and concentrate.

Cool and skim off solidified fat from the surface. Strain through a fine sieve. Clarify, if required, as described in recipe for consommé (p. 85) and use as needed.

CHICKEN STOCK

There are several ways of making good chicken stock, the choice depends on the purpose for which you want it. If you are going to serve boiled chicken as a main course and the liquid is to be served as chicken broth or consommé, then you can do no better than to put the bird, with all the giblets except the liver, to preserve the white colour of the stock, in a large pot, cover with cold water and bring to the boil. Skim off all the scum which rises to the surface until clear, then season and add sliced aromatics: 1 carrot, 1 onion, 1 leek, 1 stalk of celery and a bouquet garni.

It is a mistake to overload chicken stock with too many vegetables, because they can swamp the delicate flavour of the chicken. You may as well settle for a vegetable stock. Also, stock cooked without vegetables keeps better. Reduce heat, simmer gently for 2½–3 hours, or until the chicken is tender, depending on its age.

Take the fowl out of the stock and use as required. Skim the fat off the surface of the stock and strain through a fine strainer.

If the stock is not required for use immediately, leave to cool, then keep in a refrigerator. The fat will settle on the top and can easily be peeled off and used for cooking. If the stock is to be kept for several days, take it out of the refrigerator and bring to the boil once every 24 hours. Stock made as above will give you the basis for excellent chicken soups.

If you need chicken stock for other dishes than soup, you certainly need not go to the extravagance of using a whole fowl. Obviously, the longer the fowl is cooked in the soup, the better will be the flavour of the soup and the less flavour will be retained in the fowl.

You can make one of the following much more economical chicken stocks:–

CHICKEN CARCASS STOCK

Nowadays a chicken carcass is by no means a rare vision in the kitchen. Don't let familiarity breed contempt, never throw it away

Put the chicken carcass and giblets, if any, in a pan, cover with cold water, bring to the boil, skim, season with salt and 2 – 3 peppercorns, simmer for 2–2½ hours, strain and the stock is ready.

If you are going to use the stock immediately, you can add half the quantity of the vegetables indicated above in recipe for chicken stock. Strain, allow to cool and use as directed.

GIBLET STOCK

Whenever you are roasting a chicken or any other bird, you are bound to need a stock for the sauce or gravy. Therefore, as you remove, or unpack, the giblets, put them to cook straight away. Proceed as with any stock : put the giblets into a pan, cover with cold water, bring to the boil, skim, season, simmer for 1½–2 hours, depending on the age of the bird they came from, strain, allow to cool.

All indications given for chicken carcass or giblet stocks apply to stocks made of capon, poularde, turkey and goose.

GAME STOCK

For feathered game stock, use giblets, trimmings and bones of the appropriate bird, and follow instructions for chicken stock.

ASPIC JELLY

Any meat or bone stock can be used as a basis for aspic jelly but if the bones do not include calf's or pig's foot, it will need strengthening with gelatine. You can even make passable aspic jelly, at a pinch, by adding 15 grs (1½ oz or 1½ tablespoons) gelatine, diluted in 1½ tablespoons boiling water, to 2 dcl (½ pint or 1 cup) water with a bouillon cube added to it.

But short cuts, though admissible in emergencies, are inevitably undertaken at the expense of quality.

500 grs (1 lb) short ribs of beef
1½ kg (3 lb) shin bone
1 calf's foot
2 sliced onions
2 sliced carrots
3 tablespoons sherry (or port)
salt
2 egg whites and shells

Cut the meat into pieces, chop the bones and split the calf's foot, put into a large pan of salted cold water, slowly bring to the boil, removing the scum as it rises with a perforated spoon. Add carrot and onions, skim the surface until it is clear, cover and simmer for 3–4 hours. Strain, taste for seasoning. Chill, skim off all fat, then reheat, add sherry or port and clarify, i.e. add lightly beaten egg whites and crushed egg shells to the stock, boil it up, simmer for 15 minutes, and strain through a cloth. Cool, and use as directed.

QUICK ASPIC JELLY

- ½ litre (1 pint or 2 cups) chicken stock (p 18)
- 1 teaspoon chopped tarragon
- 2–3 sprigs parsley
- juice of 1 lemon
- 10 peppercorns
- 1 chopped shallot (or ½ onion)
- ½ bay leaf
- 30 grs (1 oz or ¼ cup) gelatine
- 3 tablespoons sherry (or Madeira)
- salt
- 1 egg white and shell

Boil the stock with tarragon, parsley, lemon juice, peppercorns, shallot and bay leaf for 10 minutes. Dissolve the gelatine in 2 tablespoons of cold water and add to the stock. Simmer for 5 minutes, add sherry and salt to taste, and strain. To clarify the jelly, bring the stock to the boil. Beat the egg white and crush the shell and add both to the stock. Simmer for 5 minutes, strain once again and use as directed.

RUSSIAN MUSHROOM STOCK

- 60 grs (2 oz) dried mushrooms
- 1 medium-sized onion
- 2 litres (2 quarts) cold water

Wash the mushrooms and soak in water for 3 hours. Bring to the boil in the same water.

Peel and quarter onion, add to mushrooms, simmer for 2–2½ hours. Strain and use as required.

The mushrooms can be used for pie fillings or, rinsed, chopped finely and served in soup.

VEGETABLE COURT-BOUILLON FOR FISH SOUPS

Allow 240 grs (8 oz or 1 cup) mirepoix of mixed vegetables, (finely shredded carrot, leek, onion and celery lightly fried in butter) to 2½ dcl (½ pint or 1 cup) dry white wine and the same amount of water. Bring to the boil with a small sprig of thyme and crushed fragment of bay leaf. Simmer to reduce by two-thirds. Enrich with a tablespoon fish fumet (p. 21), simmer for 5 minutes and use as required.

FISH FUMET

Fumet is concentrated stock made from bones and trimmings of fish.

1 kg (2 lb) bones, head and trimmings of various fish (whiting, sole, haddock, plaice, etc.)
1 chopped onion
60 grs (2 oz or ¼ cup) mushroom parings (stalks, etc.)
2 sprigs parsley
1 sprig thyme
¼ bay leaf
½ teaspoon lemon juice
pinch salt
½ litre (1 pint or 2 cups) water
2 dcl (½ pint or 1 cup) dry white wine

Put onion, mushroom parings, parsley, thyme and bay leaf in a stock pot. Cover with fish bones and trimmings, add lemon juice, season with salt, moisten with wine and water, bring to the boil, skim, then simmer gently for 30 minutes. Strain through a muslin bag.

For fish fumet made with red wine, use equal amounts of wine and water.

DASHI

The Japanese use dashi as the basis for stocks, soups, sauces and dressings. It is very easy to make and the ingredients are available in shops specialising in Oriental produce. The two vital ingredients are konbu seaweed and katsuobushi (bonito fillets) cut into shavings. In an emergency a light strained fish stock may be used.

7½ grs (¼ oz or 3 teaspoon) konbu seaweed
1 litre (1 quart) water
35 grs (1¼ oz or 5 tablespoons) katsuobushi shavings
¼ teaspoon Aji-no-Moto (monosodium glutamate)

Put konbu seaweed in a pan with water, heat and remove from heat as soon as boiling is established. Add katsuobushi, reheat, and remove from heat at the first sign of boiling. Season with Aji-no-Moto, allow to stand for 10 minutes, strain and use as required.

KVAS I

There are many varieties of this pleasant and healthy beverage. It is used as a table drink and as a basis for several kinds of borsch. It is an essential ingredient of the summer soups called okroshka (pp. 112–113). The easiest type to make is the popular kvas brewed from bread. Use rye bread, the darker the better.

To make 5–6 litres (5–6 quarts)

- 1½ kg (3 lbs) rye bread
- 5 litres (5 quarts) boiling water
- 30 grs (1 oz or 2 cakes) yeast
- 180 grs (6 oz or ¾ cup) sugar
- 60 grs (2 oz or 6 tablespoons) raisins
- 30 grs (1 oz) fresh mint leaves

Slice the bread and dry in a low oven, without allowing it to burn. Put the rusks into a large saucepan, pour in boiling water, and leave with a lid on for 3 to 4 hours. Strain, add yeast, sugar, and mint and leave to ferment for 5 to 6 hours. When foam begins to be formed on the kvas, strain it again and decant into bottles. Put several raisins into each bottle before pouring the liquid in. Cork securely : soak the corks in boiling water first to make them more elastic, and after corking the bottles, secure with string. (This is essential, because otherwise they are liable to go off with a terrible bang.) Lay the filled bottles down in a cool place (a cellar is ideal). Kvas will be ready for use in 2 to 3 days' time.

KVAS II

- 1 kg (2 lb) rye bread
- 6 litres (6 quarts) boiling water
- ½ kg (1 lb or 2 cups) treacle
- 1 tablespoon yeast
- ½ tablespoon flour
- raisins

Slice and dry the rusks as described in recipe for Kvas I. Put into a saucepan, add boiling water, cover, allow to cool, strain through a cloth but do not squeeze. Add good dark treacle and stir well to prevent it settling on the bottom. Mix the yeast with the flour and add to the liquid. Blend well, leave in a warm room for 12 hours and strain. Put two raisins into each bottle and decant the liquid into them. Cork and store as described, and the kvas will be ready for use in 2 days' time.

BÉCHAMEL SAUCE

- 60 grs (2 oz or 4 tablespoons) butter
- 2 tablespoons chopped onion (optional)
- 60 grs (2 oz or ½ cup) flour
- 1½ litre (3 pints or 6 cups) boiling milk
- ½ teaspoon salt
- 6 white peppercorns
- 2 sprigs parsley
- pinch grated nutmeg (optional)

Heat butter, add onion, cook until soft and transparent. Add flour, cook gently until it turns pale golden, gradually add milk, beating vigorously. Add salt, peppercorns, parsley and nutmeg. Simmer gently for ½ hour, stirring frequently. Cook down by one-third. Strain through a fine sieve. The above quantity will make 1 litre (2 pints or 4 cups) of creamy Béchamel. If the sauce is intended for delicately-flavoured foods, omit the onion.

MAYONNAISE

2 egg yolks
½ teaspoon salt
freshly ground black pepper
¼ teaspoon dry mustard
2 dessertspoons vinegar, or lemon juice
¼ litre (½ pint or 1 cup) olive oil

Place yolks, salt, pepper, mustard and 1 dessertspoon of vinegar (or lemon juice) in a basin. Whisk well with a fork. Change to a metal spoon and start stirring. Slowly add the oil. It is unnecessary to add it drop by drop, approximate teaspoons will work and help to do the job more quickly. Keep on stirring. It should only take about 4 minutes to blend in all the oil. Adjust seasoning and vinegar to taste.

PESTO ETTORE VIOLANI

Pesto is Ligurian green sauce, made of fresh basil, Sardo or Parmesan cheese, garlic and pine nuts. It is served with various kinds of pasta dishes and does great things for flavouring soups. The amount given below is sufficient for 4 servings of pasta. To flavour soups, add 1 tablespoon of pesto.

30 grs (1 oz or ¾ cup) fresh basil leaves
4 peeled cloves garlic
pinch salt
60 grs (2 oz or ½ cup) grated Sardo or Parmesan cheese, or a mixture of the two
2 tablespoons peeled pine nuts or walnuts
2 tablespoons butter
240 ml (½ pint or 1 cup) olive oil

Put basil, garlic, salt, cheese and nuts in a mortar and pound into paste. Little by little work in butter, then start blending in oil, a trickle at a time, as you would for mayonnaise. Keep in a screw-top jar.

CLARIFIED BUTTER

Melt the butter on a very low heat until it begins to look like olive oil and a whitish deposit forms on the bottom of the pan. Strain into a clean container and use as directed.

GARLIC BUTTER

4 cloves garlic
water

180 grs (6 oz or ¾ cup) butter

Boil garlic for 5 minutes in just enough water to cover. Drain, and pound, adding butter little by little. Rub through a sieve and store in a jar with a well-fitting lid.

Meat Soups

BEEF TEA

This makes a pleasant nourishing drink at any time but is especially valuable when there are invalids in the house, as it provides an easily digestible source of concentrated protein. It is very good for stimulating flagging appetites. There are special screw-top marmites in which the beef is sealed and which are placed in a pan of boiling water for an hour then strained, but it is simple to make in an ordinary double saucepan.

1½ kg (3 lb) lean beef (shin or round)
1 litre (2 pints or 4 cups) cold water
salt

Wash and dry the meat, remove all fat and skin. Scrape, mince or chop the meat finely. Add water, stir, cover and leave to stand for 20 – 30 minutes. Put to cook in a double saucepan, cover, simmer for 2½ – 3 hours, stirring from time to time. Strain, season, chill and skim off any fat. To serve, heat in a cup placed in hot water, adding more salt if necessary.

POT-AU-FEU

This is a great French soup which provides a delicious broth and a splendid main course of boiled beef. The amounts indicated below will provide at least 2 meals for 6 persons.

2½ kg (5 lbs) beef with bones (round, chuck or rib)
1 bunch carrots
360 grs (12 oz) turnips
1 bunch leeks
1 tablespoon salt
1 stalk celery
1 medium-sized onion
1 clove garlic
2 cloves
1 sprig thyme
½ bay leaf
5 litres (5 quarts) cold water

Put the meat, tied with string, and the bones into a large pot. Add water and salt. Bring to a boil slowly, skim off the scum which rises to the surface. Repeat this skimming operation 2 or 3 times, adding a few tablespoons of cold water each time to slow down the boiling process. Add the vegetables and other ingredients, bring to the boil once more, cover with a lid and simmer gently for at least 4 hours.

If young vegetables are used, add them to the stockpot after the meat has been cooking for 2 hours. Slow cooking of the Pot-au-feu ensures a clean, savory taste and good amber colour.

To serve, skim off surplus fat, taste for seasoning, add more salt if necessary, and strain the broth into a soup tureen.

Serve the meat and vegetables separately with a sauce, grated horseradish or mustard.

The Pot-au-feu provides meat stock, which is the basis of many soups, sauces and other culinary preparations. Before storing for future use, strain through a fine strainer to remove vegetable particles which cause rapid fermentation. Store in an earthenware or enamelled container. Bring to a boil before using.

The use of cabbage in Pot-au-feu is not recommended. It promotes too active a fermentation and reduces the keeping quality of the stock.

MINESTRONE

This is one of the great soups of the world and there are as many variations as there are cooks. A really good Italian minestrone should have a foundation of salt pork or gammon and white haricot beans. A great variety of other ingredients are added, including all kinds of vegetables and pasta, and it should be served with a sprinkling of finely grated Parmesan cheese.

6 Servings

- 240 grs (8 oz or 1 cup) white haricot beans
- 1 finely chopped onion
- 2 crushed cloves of garlic
- 1–2 tablespoons pork fat
- ½ kg (1 lb or 2 cups) diced salt pork or raw gammon
- 2 litres (2 quarts or 8 cups) stock or water
- bouquet garni
- 1½ tablespoons chopped parsley
- 2 medium diced carrots
- 1 small shredded cabbage
- 180 grs (6 oz or 1½ cups) peeled chopped tomatoes
- 120 grs (4 oz or ½ cup) shelled peas
- 90 grs (3 oz) sliced French beans
- 4 tablespoons rice or small type pasta (pastina, stars, alphabet, etc)
- salt and freshly grated black pepper
- 1 teaspoon finely chopped basil
- grated Parmesan cheese or 1 tablespoon pesto (p 23)

Soak the beans in cold water overnight.

In a big saucepan fry onion and garlic in pork fat until soft. Add pork, stock and bouquet garni. Bring to the boil. Drain and add beans and simmer gently for 1½ hours. Add parsley and carrots and cook for 20 minutes. Add cabbage, tomatoes, peas, French beans and rice or pasta. Cook for 15–20 minutes. If using pasta, simmer until it is just *al dente,* i.e. firm to the teeth. Remove bouquet garni, season to taste, add basil or pesto and serve with grated Parmesan cheese.

MEAT BORSCH

Borsch quite deservedly is classed in the gastronomical world with about a dozen of really great soups.

It is a good plan to make a double amount of Borsch required for it is one of those soups which taste even better on the second day. To enhance the colour, add some fresh beetroot as described. Serve with pirozhki (pp. 133–135).

8 Servings

- 750 gr (1½ lb) stewing beef
- 2½ litres (2½ quarts) water
- ½ kg (1 lb) white cabbage
- 3–4 beetroots
- 2 carrots
- 1 parsnip
- 2 stalks celery
- 1 large onion
- 4 tablespoons tomato purée
- 1 tablespoon sugar
- 1 tablespoon red wine vinegar
- 1–2 bay leaves
- 1½ teaspoons salt
- ½ teaspoon ground black pepper
- 4–5 whole Allspice seeds
- 1 tablespoon lemon juice
- 1 tablespoon chopped dill
- 1 tablespoon chopped parsley
- sour cream

Wash and dry the meat, trim off surplus fat, cut into pieces and put in a saucepan with water. Bring to the boil, skim off any scum which rises to the surface, reduce heat, cover and simmer for 45 minutes. Reserve one beetroot. Shred the cabbage and cut all root vegetables first into slices then into 'matchsticks'. Quarter the onion and slice thinly. Add all vegetables to stock and continue to simmer for 20 to 25 minutes. Add tomato purée, vinegar, sugar, bay leaf, salt, pepper and Allspice. Cook for 15 minutes on low heat, check seasoning, sharpen with lemon juice, sprinkle with chopped dill and parsley and serve piping hot with sour cream.

To ensure the characteristic attractive rich colour of Borsch, keep one beetroot for last minute use. Grate it finely, put in a small pan with a cupful of stock, simmer for 5 minutes and strain into the Borsch.

SHCHI

This, after borsch, is perhaps the most popular of Russian soups. It is practically unknown in the Western world, except in Paris restaurants which pride themselves on their Russian menus. My English and American friends die laughing when I tell them the name of this soup, though it is no funnier than the Italian for 'ski'. They say it sounds like a badly controlled sneeze. However, the soup is not to be sneezed at!

Shchi requires good beef, fish or mushroom stock. The meat shchi is cooked with fresh white cabbage and is one of the ways of restoring to this excellent vegetable its place in good eating.

These soups share one admirable quality with borsch. You can make them in advance or in a bigger quantity, for they invariably taste better on the second day, due to something mysterious in the cabbage chemistry.

Shchi based on fish stock are more often made with pickled cabbage (sauerkraut). A portion of meat or fish is served in each plate of shchi.

This soup is also made of spinach, sorrel and young nettles. It is usual to serve shchi with fresh or sour cream, hard-boiled eggs and finely chopped dill or parsley. The classical accompaniments to shchi made of fresh cabbage are sour cream, cream cheese tartlets or pirozhki (pp. 133–135), to shchi made of pickled cabbage, fresh cream, kasha, buckwheat pirozhki or croûtons. I personally prefer sour cream with both kinds of shchi.

As for borsch, all vegetables for shchi are normally cut into uniform strips, but there is one type, called lazy shchi, because the cabbage is in portion-sized wedges. Here is the recipe.

LAZY SHCHI

6–8 Servings

- 2 litres (2 quarts or 8 cups) beef or veal stock (p 17)
- 750 grs ($1\frac{1}{2}$ lb) good white cabbage
- 1 large onion
- 1–2 leeks, white part only
- 1–2 tablespoons buttter
- 1 stalk celery
- $\frac{1}{2}$ medium sized parsnip
- 2 medium sized carrots
- 5–6 peppercorns
- 1 bay leaf
- 1 tablespoon flour
- salt
- 2–3 ripe, peeled, sliced tomatoes
- buckwheat pirozhki (p 134–135) or cream cheese tartlets (p 140)
- sour cream
- 1 tablespoon chopped dill

Strain stock, remove all surface fat. Cut cabbage into quarters, leave to soak in cold water for 1 hour. Chop onion and leeks finely. In a large saucepan melt 1 tablespoon butter or fat skimmed off the stock, fry onion and leeks until soft and pale golden.

Cut cabbage into 6–8 portions, drop into boiling water, bring to the boil, drain and add to onion and leek. Do not stir, so as not to break up the cabbage wedges. It is their unshred shape and size which gives the shchi its name. Add enough stock to cover, bring to the boil, simmer for 10 minutes.

Meanwhile, shred celery, parsnip and carrots, blanch in boiling water for 2 minutes, drain and add to cabbage with peppercorns and bay leaf.

Melt remaining butter and fry flour, stirring to mix well but without allowing the roux to brown. Gradually dilute with a cupful of stock, bring to the boil, stir and strain into soup. Add the rest of the stock, season with salt to taste, add tomatoes, simmer for 10 minutes and serve piping hot with pirozhki or cream cheese tartlets. Add a tablespoon of sour cream to each plate and sprinkle with dill.

PICKLED CABBAGE SHCHI

6–8 Servings

- 1 litre (1 quart) mushroom stock (p 20)
- 1 litre (1 quart) beef stock (p 17)
- ½ kg (1 lb) pickled cabbage (sauerkraut)
- 2 tablespoons butter
- 1 medium sized finely chopped onion
- 1 tablespoon flour
- 6–8 peppercorns
- 1 bay leaf
- salt
- 120 ml (4 oz or ½ cup) double cream or sour cream
- blinchiki (p 136) or
- kasha (p 150) or
- buckwheat croûtons (p 140)

Prepare mushroom stock, rinse and slice mushrooms. Strain beef stock and remove all surface fat. Squeeze all liquid out of pickled cabbage and keep it. If the cabbage is very sour, scald with boiling water in a collander and squeeze out by pressing with a wooden spoon. Melt 1 tablespoon of butter and fry onion until soft. Add pickled cabbage and fry, stirring frequently, for 10 minutes. Leave on lowest possible heat and do not allow to brown.

In another pan, melt remaining butter and fry flour, without browning. Dilute the roux (mixture of flour and butter) with 2½ dcl (½ pint or 1 cup) mushroom stock, blending it in gradually, strain over cabbage. Transfer to a large saucepan, add peppercorns, bay leaf, mushrooms and all the stock. Bring to the boil, cover and simmer gently for 1 hour. Season with salt. Taste the shchi and if not sharp enough add reserved pickled cabbage liquor. Remove from heat, stir in cream and serve piping hot with blinchiki, kasha or buckwheat croûtons.

SIBERIAN PELMENI

The great point about this Siberian version of wun tun is that they can be prepared days in advance and kept in the freezer. Siberians say that pelmeni taste better as a result of such preliminary freezing. It is a recognised custom among good Siberian housewives to keep several hundred pelmeni in their cold cellars, just in case an unexpected crowd of hungry guests drop in. Refrigeration is no problem. Those who have no cellars hang pillowcases full of pelmeni outside their windows and the temperature does the rest.

6 Servings

- ½ kg (1 lb or 2 cups) best minced beef
- 1 finely chopped onion
- salt and pepper
- iced water
- noodle paste (p 154)
- 1½ kg (3 pints or 6 cups) strained beef stock or consommé (p 85)

Mix minced beef (or a mixture of beef and lean pork) with onion and season to taste. Add 2–3 tablespoons iced water and mix well.

Roll out the noodle paste very thin, cut out small circles with a pastry cutter, put a little meat filling on each circlet of pastry, crimp up the edges, forming rather a plump semi-circle and join the two tapering ends together, pinching hard to make them stick. Continue until all pelmeni are done, putting them on a lightly floured board, without allowing them to touch.

Drop pelmeni a few at a time into boiling stock, allowing boiling to be re-established before adding any more. Simmer gently for 10 minutes or until pelmeni float up to the surface. Serve in the soup, with a sprinkling of chopped dill or parsley. Siberians like their pelmeni with a dressing made of 2 teaspoons of mustard diluted with 3–4 tablespoons of wine vinegar.

Leftover boiled pelmeni are delicious fried in a little butter.

RUSSIAN CHESTNUT SOUP WITH VEAL QUENELLES

6 Servings

- ½ kg (1 lb) chestnuts, shelled and peeled (p 102)
- 1 litre (2 pints or 4 cups) stock
- salt and pepper
- 2 slices white bread, with crusts cut off
- a little milk
- 1 small chopped onion
- 2 tablespoons butter
- 240 grs (8 oz or 1 cup) minced veal
- pinch nutmeg
- 120 ml (4 oz or ½ cup) cream
- 1 beaten egg
- 2–3 tablespoons sherry
- 2 raw yolks

Simmer peeled chestnuts in enough stock to cover until they begin to break up. Rub through a sieve or pass through a blender, adding remainder of stock. Season and taste.

Soak bread with enough milk to cover. Fry onion in 1 tablespoon butter until soft and transparent, add to veal. Squeeze out surplus milk from the bread and add bread to veal. Season with salt, pepper and nutmeg. Add 1 tablespoon of cream and beaten egg. Blend well, roll quenelle mixture into a sausage, wrap in muslin, secure with thread. Drop into salted boiling water, simmer for 6–7 minutes. Remove carefully, allow to cool, unwrap, cut into diagonal slices and keep warm. Reheat soup. Add sherry. Dilute yolks with remaining cream. Remove soup from heat. Stir in yolks and cream mixture, garnish soup with quenelles and serve.

SPANISH COCIDO

Cocido is a traditional dish and, at times, by its consistency it comes nearer to 'stew' than to 'soup'.

6 Servings

- 500 grs (1 lb) beef
- a bone, or bones (up to 240 grs – ½ lb – in weight)
- 180 grs (6 oz) salt pork
- 60 grs (2 oz) bacon
- 2½ litres (2½ quarts) water
- 240 grs (8 oz or 1¼ cups) chick-peas (soaked overnight)
- 2 carrots
- 2 leeks
- 60 grs (2 oz) chorizo (Spanish pork sausage which can be found in Continental shops)
- 1 head of white cabbage (or 2 of lettuce)
- salt and pepper

Place the meat, the bones, the pork and the bacon into hot water; when it comes to the boil, skim the surface and add the chick-peas, the carrots and the leeks (whole) and 10 minutes later a few slices of chorizo. Season with salt and pepper to taste. Cover and cook slowly for 3 hours. Strain and keep the stock. The meat with the chick-peas and all the other ingredients with which it was cooked, serve as a main dish.

With this cocido it is usual to serve a whole head of cabbage (the small, tight, white variety) or 2 heads of lettuce, cooked in a small quantity of salted water with a couple of slices of bacon laid on top to flavour it. Do not cook for longer than 12 to 15 minutes. Then strain and serve.

This is a rather nourishing cocido – a very good and sustaining winter dish.

GALICIAN POTE

6–8 Servings

- 1 bone
- 60 grs (2 oz) of bacon
- 60 grs (2 oz) of chorizo
- 480 grs (1 lb) salted pork (soaked overnight) (pigs' trotters, head or ox-tail can be used if preferred)
- 240 grs (8 oz or 1¼ cups) of white kidney beans (soaked overnight)
- 480 grs (1 lb) fresh leg of pork
- 1 small white cabbage
- 1½ kg (3 lb) potatoes (small size)

Put all the ingredients into a large saucepan, except potatoes, chorizo and cabbage, and cover with water. Simmer for 2 hours. Slice cabbage and chorizo and add to stock. Cook for another hour then add whole peeled potatoes. When the potatoes are done, take 2 or 3 out, and mash them. Take out the meat, chorizo and potatoes and keep hot, to serve as a main dish. Put mashed potato back into the broth to thicken it. Serve the pote with the cabbage and the beans.

SCOTCH BROTH

6 Servings

- 90 grs (3 oz or 7½ tablespoons) pearl barley
- 2½ litres (2½ quarts) water
- 1 scrag end of lamb, roughly chopped
- 2 onions
- bouquet garni
- 1 tablespoon butter
- 120 grs (4 oz or ½ cup) diced carrot
- 120 grs (4 oz or ½ cup) diced turnip
- 3–4 shredded stalks celery
- salt and pepper
- 1 tablespoon chopped parsley

Soak barley in enough cold water to cover overnight. Put the lamb in a pan with water, bring to the boil and remove scum.

Peel the onions, wash the peel and add to pan, together with bouquet garni. Peel adds to the richness of colour. Simmer 1½ hours.

Chop the onion finely and fry lightly in butter, without allowing it to brown. Extract bouquet garni and onion peel from the pan. Put in onions, carrot, turnip and celery. Simmer for 30 minutes.

Take the meat out of the broth. Remove and discard all bones. Shred the meat and put back into pan. Drain barley and add to broth. Season to taste, simmer for 1 hour. Just before serving, sprinkle with chopped parsley.

BROTCHAN ROY/IRISH LEEK SOUP

4 Servings

- 1 kg (2 lb) leeks
- 1 litre (1 quart) stock
- 1 tablespoon butter
- 2 tablespoons oatmeal flakes
- salt and pepper
- pinch nutmeg
- 4 bacon rashers
- 1 tablespoon chopped parsley
- 2–3 tablespoons cream

Wash and cut up leeks. Heat stock, add butter. Bring to the boil, add oatmeal and boil fast for 2 minutes. Add leeks, season with salt, pepper and nutmeg, cover and simmer for 1 hour.

Fry or grill the bacon rashers until crisp and crumbly, keep warm. Add parsley to soup, simmer for a couple of minutes, remove from heat, blend in cream. Serve at once with topping of crumbled bacon.

BALTIC RICE AND LEMON SOUP

6 Servings

- 4 tablespoons cooked rice
- $2\frac{1}{2}$ litres ($2\frac{1}{2}$ quarts) stock
- seasoning
- juice of $\frac{1}{2}$ lemon
- 1 sliced lemon
- 1–2 tablespoons chopped dill

Bring rice to the boil in seasoned stock. Add lemon juice and simmer for 2–3 minutes. Drop in lemon slices, simmer on lowest possible heat for 5 minutes. Sprinkle with dill and serve. If dill is not available, use parsley.

PHILADELPHIA PEPPER POT SOUP

6 Servings

- 3–4 shredded rashers bacon
- 1 chopped onion
- 2 sliced leeks
- 3 chopped stalks celery
- 1 seeded diced green pepper
- 3 tablespoons butter
- 2 tablespoons flour
- $1\frac{1}{2}$ litres (3 pints or 6 cups) stock
- I dozen crushed peppercorns
- salt
- pinch cayenne pepper
- 2 tablespoons cream
- $1\frac{1}{2}$ tablespoons chopped parsley

Fry bacon, onion, leeks, celery and green pepper in butter until soft, stirring frequently and keeping the pan on low heat. Sprinkle in flour, cook while stirring for 5 minutes, without browning. Gradually add stock, stir, add peppercorns, salt to taste and cayenne pepper. Bring to the boil, simmer for 30 minutes. Remove from heat, stir in cream. Sprinkle with parsley and serve. 1 or 2 large diced potatoes may be added to this soup to make it more substantial.

PUCHERO

This is a super stew of Argentine origin which provides three dishes in one. The stock makes excellent soup, the meat is served with mustard and the vegetables, in as great a variety as the season or pocket permits, make a third dish.

6 Servings

- $1\frac{1}{2}$ kg (3 lb) beef shank
- 2 onions
- 2 carrots
- 2 leeks
- 2 stalks celery
- several sprigs parsley
- 1 bay leaf
- 1 small white cabbage
- 3 corn cobs
- 6 potatoes
- salt and pepper

Cut the meat into portions and put in a big saucepan with 3 litres (3 quarts) salted boiling water. Skim until the surface is clear. Peel and quarter onions and carrots, trim leeks and cut in half lengthwise, cut celery into chunks. Add all these vegetables and parsley to the meat, allow to come to the boil again, then reduce heat and simmer on very low heat for $1\frac{1}{2}$ hours. Cut cabbage into 6 wedges, corn cobs into 5 cm (2 inch) chunks. Peel and quarter potatoes.

Add this second lot of vegetables to the puchero. Season to taste, simmer until all vegetables are tender.

BOLIVIAN CHUPE

This is one of many substantial South American dishes, more stews than soups, usually served as a first course. The chilli dressing which is added to the soup can be fiercely hot, so the amount of chilli used should be adjusted to suit individual tastes.

6 Servings

- 750 gr ($1\frac{1}{2}$ lbs) lean beef
- 240 grs (8 oz) peeled diced carrot
- 3 tablespoons shredded celery
- $\frac{1}{2}$ kg (1 lb) peeled diced potatoes
- 125 grs (4 oz or $\frac{3}{4}$ cup) sweet corn
- 125 grs (4 ozs or $\frac{3}{4}$ cup) shelled peas
- salt and pepper
- 120 grs (4 oz or $\frac{1}{2}$ cup) oil
- 1 small chopped onion
- 2 tablespoons chilli powder

Put the meat in a pan with 3 litres (3 quarts) water, bring to the boil, skim until the surface is free of all scum. Add carrot and cook for 30 minutes. Add celery, potatoes and corn, and simmer for 30 minutes. Add peas, season to taste with salt and pepper and simmer for 10–15 minutes.

Heat oil and fry the onion until soft. Dilute chilli powder with equal amount of cold water, stir the mixture into the pan with the onion and cook together. The chilli should colour the oil but not emulsify with it. Keep hot.

Take the meat out of the soup and dice. Put back in the soup, heat through and serve. Hand the chilli dressing separately to be added to soup at table.

TYROLEAN SOUP

6 Servings

- 2 tablespoons butter
- 2 finely chopped onions
- 1½ tablespoons flour
- 1 litre (2 pints or 4 cups) stock
- 4 tablespoons red wine
- 2 eggs beaten
- 1 tablespoon chopped parsley
- 1 tablespoon chopped chives
- salt and pepper
- 120 ml (4 oz or ½ cup) cream

Heat butter in a saucepan and lightly brown onions. Stir in flour and cook a pale golden roux. Gradually stir in stock, bring to the boil, simmer for 15 minutes. Add wine. Whisk eggs with parsley and chives. Remove soup from heat, blend in eggs, season to taste. Reheat gently without allowing the soup to boil. Add cream and serve.

KRUPNIK

This is Polish barley soup, a substantial one and frequently served as a meal in itself.

6 Servings

- 90 grs (3 oz or 1 cup) pearl barley
- cold water
- 2 litres (2 quarts) meat stock
- 2 tablespoons oil
- 2 sliced onions
- 2 diced carrots
- 1 diced parsnip
- 3 stalks shredded celery
- 2–3 diced potatoes
- 60 grs (2 oz or ¾ cup) diced fresh mushrooms (or 7–8 dried mushrooms)
- 1 bay leaf
- salt and pepper
- chopped dill

Soak barley in water overnight. Drain. Cook in ½ litre (1 pint or 2 cups) stock for 1½ hours.

In a big pan heat oil and lightly fry onion, add barley and the liquid in which it has been simmering, the rest of the stock, carrots, parsnip, celery, potatoes, mushrooms and bay leaf. Cover and simmer for 30 minutes. Season to taste with salt and pepper. Serve garnished with chopped dill. If fresh dill is not available, use parsley.

PERSIAN ALMOND SOUP

6 Servings

- 1 kilo (2 lb) lean veal
- 2 litres (2 quarts) cold water
- 1 medium sized onion
- 1–2 stalks celery
- 1 bay leaf
- 4–5 white peppercorns
- 1–1½ teaspoons salt
- rind and juice of 1 lemon
- 240 gr (8 oz 2⅔ cups) ground almonds
- 6 hard boiled eggs, shelled
- 6 bitter almonds, blanched
- pinch verbena salt

Put the veal in a saucepan, add water, bring to the boil. Skim any scum which rises to the surface. Cover and simmer for 1 hour.

Chop onion and shred celery, add to stock, together with bay leaf, peppercorns and salt. Cook for 1½ hours. Chop the lemon rind finely. Add half of it and all the lemon juice to the stock. Continue to simmer for another hour. Strain the stock, leave until cold, then remove all surface fat. Put the ground almonds into a mortar. Halve hard-boiled eggs, remove yolks and add to almonds, together with bitter almonds. Keep the whites of egg and use for another dish, as stuffing or garnish.

Season the almonds in the mortar with verbena salt, add remaining chopped lemon rind and pound to a paste. Dilute with a cupful of stock, adding it little by little.

Bring the rest of the stock to the boil. Add pounded almond mixture, blend thoroughly, simmer for 10 minutes and serve.

HOT AND SOUR BEAN CURD SOUP

4 Servings

- 4 dried Chinese mushrooms
- 240 grs (8 oz or 1 cup) thinly sliced lean pork
- 2 tablespoons shelled peas
- 90 grs (3 oz) thinly sliced bean curd
- 1 litre (2 pints or 4 cups) boiling stock
- 1 tablespoon Shao Shing Chinese wine or dry sherry
- 2 tablespoons soya sauce
- 2 tablespoons vinegar
- 1 teaspoon salt
- ½ teaspoon pepper
- 1 tablespoon cornflour
- 2 tablespoons cold water

Soak mushrooms in water for 2 hours, remove stalks and shred. Put mushrooms, pork, peas and bean curd into a saucepan, add boiling stock and simmer for 12–15 minutes, until pork is cooked. Add shao shing, soya sauce, vinegar, salt and pepper, simmer for 1 minute.

Dilute cornflour with water, stir into the soup, simmer for a couple of minutes, stirring, until the soup thickens and serve.

PEKIN SOUP

6 Servings

- 3–4 Chinese dried mushrooms
- 120 grs (4 oz or ½ cup) lean pork, cut in thin strips
- 120 grs (4 oz or ½ cup) breast of chicken, cut in thin strips
- 1 tablespoon peanut oil
- 240 grs (8 oz or ⅔ cup) shredded Chinese cabbage or celery
- ¾ litre (1½ pints or 6 cups) stock
- 1 teaspoon finely chopped fresh ginger
- 1 tablespoon shao shing Chinese wine or sherry
- 1 teaspoon soya sauce
- ½ teaspoon salt

Soak the mushrooms in cold water for 2–3 hours, remove stalk and shred. Heat oil in a large saucepan and fry pork and chicken until they change colour. Add Chinese cabbage and shredded mushrooms and fry together, stirring, for 2–3 minutes.

Bring stock to the boil, add to fried ingredients, simmer for 2 minutes. Add remaining ingredients, simmer for 6–7 minutes and serve.

MALAYAN BEEF AND PRAWN SOUP

4 Servings

- ½ kg (1 lb) lean beef
- water
- 3 onions
- 2 cloves garlic
- 2½ cm (1 inch) piece fresh ginger
- ¾ teaspoon ground turmeric
- 1 teaspoon ground coriander
- 240 grs (8 oz or 1¼ cup) prawns
- 3 tablespoons butter
- salt
- 1 tablespoon fresh lime juice

Put the beef in a saucepan with 1 litre (2 pints or 4 cups) cold water. Cut one onion into quarters, crush one clove of garlic and add to beef. Bring to the boil, leave to simmer for 1 hour.

Mince second onion, pound in a mortar with remaining clove of garlic, ginger, turmeric and coriander.

Cut the prawns into pieces and fry in 2 tablespoons butter for 2 minutes. Add pounded onion and slices of prawns, fry stirring for 3–4 minutes.

With a perforated spoon extract boiled onion and garlic from soup and discard. Add prawn and onion mixture to soup, simmer until beef is quite tender. Take the beef out, slice and return to soup. Season to taste. Slice the third onion into rings and fry until crisp in remaining butter.

Add lime juice to soup. If fresh limes are not available, use lemon juice.

Pour soup into a serving tureen or individual bowls, sprinkle with onion rings and serve.

FRENCH OX-TAIL SOUP

6 Servings

- 750 kg (1½ lb) ox-tail
- flour
- 2–3 tablespoons oil
- 1 chopped onion
- 1 chopped carrot
- 240 grs (8 oz or ⅔ cup) shredded celery
- 1½ litre (3 pints or 6 cups) water
- 1 bay leaf
- 1 tablespoon washed pearl barley
- 1 teaspoon salt
- ½ teaspoon pepper
- 120 ml (4 oz or ½ cup) red wine
- 2 tablespoons chopped parsley

Chop the ox-tail into joints, roll in flour and brown in hot oil. Add onion, carrot, celery, water, bay leaf, and barley. Bring to the boil, simmer for 2 hours. Season with salt and pepper and continue to simmer for another hour. Take the tails out, bone and put the meat back in the soup. Add wine, simmer for 5 minutes, sprinkle with parsley and serve.

NIGERIAN SOUP

4 Servings

- 120 grs (4 oz or 1 cup) roasted peanuts
- ¾ litre (1½ pints or 3 cups) stock
- 1–2 finely chopped red chillis
- 1 finely chopped onion
- 1 finely chopped green pepper
- salt
- juice of ½ lemon

Crush the nuts into flour; do not over-pound to avoid turning them into peanut butter. Heat stock. Dilute peanuts with 1 cup of the stock. Stir the mixture into the rest of the hot stock. Add chillis, onion and green pepper. Season with salt to taste. Simmer until the soup thickens and the onion is soft. Add lemon juice, stir and serve.

SHURPA/TURKMENIAN SOUP

6 Servings

- 750 grs (1½ lb) lean beef
- 2 sliced onions
- 2 tablespoons butter
- 2 large diced carrots
- 240 grs (8 oz or 1¾ cups) peeled chopped tomatoes
- 1½ litres (3 pints or 6 cups) stock
- ½ kg (1 lb or 2 cups) peeled diced potatoes
- 1 teaspoon chopped fresh basil
- 1 teaspoon salt
- ½ teaspoon freshly ground black pepper
- 1½ tablespoons chopped dill (or parsley)

Cut the meat into 2½ cm (1 inch) squares. In a large saucepan fry onions in butter until soft. Add meat and brown lightly.

Add carrots and tomatoes and continue to cook, stirring, for 5 minutes. Pour in stock, bring to the boil. Add potatoes, basil, salt and pepper. Simmer for 20–25 minutes. Sprinkle with dill and serve.

CAUCASIAN KHARCHO

6 Servings

- 750 grs (1½ lb) mutton, cut from the leg
- 1½ litres (3 pints or 6 cups) water
- 2 chopped onions
- 2 crushed cloves garlic
- 100 grs (3½ oz or ½ cup) rice
- 120 grs (4 oz or ¾ cup) damsons
- salt and pepper
- 1 tablespoon butter
- 120 grs (4 oz or ¾ cup) peeled chopped tomatoes
- 1½ tablespoons chopped dill

Cut the meat into pieces allowing 3 or 4 pieces per portion. Put in a large saucepan, cover with water, bring to the boil, skim off all scum which rises to the surface, cover and simmer for 1½ hours.

Add onion and garlic. Wash rice until the water runs clear, add to soup. Bring to the boil, add damsons and season to taste. Simmer for 30 minutes.

Heat butter, or fat skimmed off the soup, and fry tomatoes until they are reduced to paste. Add to soup, cook for 5 minutes, check seasoning, sprinkle with dill and serve.

RASSOLNIK/RUSSIAN KIDNEY AND DILL PICKLE SOUP

6 Servings

- 1½ litres (3 pints or 6 cups) consommé (p 85)
- ½ kg (1 lb) veal or lamb kidney
- 1 parsnip
- 2 stalks celery
- 3 medium-sized potatoes
- 240 grs (8 oz) dill cucumbers
- 2 tablespoons butter
- 1 chopped onion
- 1 bay leaf
- 120 grs (4 oz) sorrel or lettuce
- 1½ dcl (4 oz or ½ cup) brine in which cucumbers were pickled
- salt and freshly ground black pepper
- 1½ dcl (4 oz or ½ cup) sour cream
- 2 tablespoons chopped fresh dill or parsley

Prepare consommé, remove all surface fat. Trim kidneys, remove all fat and membranes, cut each kidney in 3–4 pieces and wash thoroughly. Put in a saucepan, cover with cold water, bring to the boil. Drain, rinse, put in fresh cold water and simmer for 1 hour.

Peel and cut parsnip into matchsticks. Shred celery, peel and dice potatoes. Slice the cucumbers. The best cucumbers for this soup are home-pickled in brine with dill for 3 days, but there are quite good dill cucumbers sold in delicatessen shops which do very well. Just make sure that they are pickled in brine and not in vinegar.

Heat butter in large saucepan and gently fry onion, parsnip and celery, to soften, but do not allow to brown. Add cucumbers, potatoes, stock and bay leaf. Bring to the boil, simmer for 15 minutes.

Shred sorrel and add to soup. Pour in cucumber brine. Drain the kidneys, slice and add to soup. Check seasoning, add more salt if necessary, grind in pepper to taste. Serve piping hot, topped with a dollop of sour cream and sprinkled with dill.

EREVAN BOSBASH/ARMENIAN PEA SOUP WITH APPLE AND PRUNES

6 Servings

750 grs (1½ lb) lean lamb
2 litres (2 quarts) stock
120 grs (4 oz or 1 cup) prunes
1 finely chopped onion
2 tablespoons butter
½ kg (1 lb or 2 cups) shelled peas
2 medium-sized apples
1–2 tablespoons tomato purée
salt
1–2 chopped red chillis

Cut lamb into portions and boil in stock until tender. Take meat out, cool stock and remove surface grease. Soak prunes in enough cold water to cover, drain and remove stones.

Gently cook onion in butter until soft and transparent. Bring stock to the boil, add onion and peas and simmer until tender.

Peel and slice apples and add to soup together with prunes. Stir in tomato purée, add meat, season to taste with salt and chillis, simmer for 10 minutes and serve.

ARMENIAN MUTTON AND AUBERGINE SOUP

6 Servings

750 grs (1½ lb) lean mutton
2 litres (2 quarts) stock
2–3 tablespoons butter
2 medium-sized chopped onions
240 grs (8 oz) sliced aubergines
240 grs (8 oz) peeled, sliced tomatoes
120 grs (4 oz) French beans
2–3 medium-sized peeled diced potatoes
1 seeded shredded green pepper
salt and black pepper
2 tablespoons lemon juice
2 tablespoons chopped parsley

Cut the mutton into portions, cook in stock until tender, remove. Strain, cool and de-grease stock.

Heat butter in a big saucepan and brown the pieces of mutton. Add onion and fry together until the onions become soft.

Add aubergines, tomatoes, beans, potatoes and green pepper and fry for 3–4 minutes.

Pour in stock, bring to the boil, season to taste, add lemon juice and simmer until vegetables are tender.

Do not overcook.

Sprinkle with parsley and serve.

KO-OUM KOOK KOREAN BEEF AND TURNIP SOUP

6 Servings

1 kg (2 lb) shin of beef
2 litres (2 quarts) cold water
240 grs (½ lb) young turnips
1 teaspoon black pepper

1 tablespoon sesame seeds
1 teaspoon salt
1–2 cloves garlic
1 medium-size red pepper
6 spring onions
1 tablespoon light soya sauce
small pinch Ve-Tsin

Wash and dry the beef, trim off surplus fat, put into a saucepan, cover with water and leave to stand for half an hour. Bring to the boil, skim until no more scum rises to the surface. Peel turnips and add to the soup. Season with freshly ground black pepper, cover, reduce heat to the minimum and simmer very gently for 2½ hours.

'Parch' sesame seeds, i.e. heat, stirring in a pan without any fat until they begin to jump. Then pound with salt.

Chop garlic, red pepper and spring onions. Remove beef, cut into cubes, sprinkle with salt and sesame seed, garlic, red pepper, spring onions, soya sauce and Ve-Tsin. Mix well in a soup tureen and leave to stand for 10 minutes for the spices to flavour the meat. Keep hot over a pan of simmering water. Reheat soup with the turnips, pour it over the beef and serve.

MOLAGU-TUNNI / MULLIGATAWNY

Garam-masala (p. 150) is an essential ingredient of mulligatawny soup and of most curry dishes, a mixture of spices which gives curries their flavours. Indian cooks do not buy commercial curry powder, they prefer to grind and blend their own mixtures. It is usual for housewives to prepare it fresh daily.

4 Servings

180 grs (6 oz or ⅞ cup) dhal (lentils)
2 onions
1 bay leaf
water
1 clove garlic
1½ tablespoons ghee
1 tablespoon garam-masala (see p 150)
1¼ litres (2½ pints or 5 cups) stock
salt
4–5 tablespoons coconut cream (see p 151)
1 lemon

Pick over dhal (lentils), wash, put in a bowl, cover with cold water and leave to soak for 1½ to 2 hours.

Slice one onion. Drain dhal, put in a saucepan with onion, bay leaf and ½ litre (1 pint or 2 cups) water. Bring to the boil, reduce heat and simmer until dhal is soft, then rub through a sieve or pass through a blender. Chop remaining onion and garlic.

In a saucepan big enough to take all ingredients, fry chopped onion and garlic gently in ghee until soft. Add garam-masala, cook stirring 2–3 minutes. Add dhal, mix well, stir in stock, season to taste, bring to the boil and simmer for a few minutes to heat through. Just before serving, blend in coconut cream. Slice lemon and serve separately.

SPANISH POTATO, HAM AND EGG SOUP

6 Servings

- 1½ litres (1½ quarts) stock
- 2–3 medium-size potatoes
- 2 eggs
- 90 grs (3 oz or 6 tablespoons) ham
- salt and pepper

Bring stock to the boil. Peel and wash the potatoes, cook, mash them well and add to the stock. Boil the eggs, take out yolks, mash them. Chop up the whites and the ham. Add to the soup, season to taste, stir well and serve.

OX-TAIL AND GREEN PEA SOUP

6 Servings

- 1 kg (2 lb) ox-tail
- 480 grs (1 lb or 2 cups) green peas
- 3 leeks
- 3 carrots
- 1 bay leaf
- salt and pepper
- 1 teaspoon sugar

Wash the ox-tail and put it into a saucepan with 3 litres (6 pints or 12 cups) of water. Bring to the boil and leave simmering, skimming frequently. Simmer for 2 hours, pour off a little of the stock and cook the peas in it for 3–4 minutes, so that they just soften a little, then remove from heat. Scrape, clean and wash the leeks and the carrots, slice them and with a bay leaf add to the ox-tail. Cook together for an hour, season, then strain. Burn the sugar in a clean frying-pan and add it to the soup to give it a nice golden colour. Take the meat off the bones, cut it neatly and put into a soup tureen together with the peas. Pour in the strained soup and serve.

ROSITA SOUP

6 Servings

- 1½ litres (1½ quarts) stock
- salt and pepper
- 6 tablespoons tapioca or semolina
- 90 grs (3 oz or 6 tablespoons) veal or pork
- 60 grs (2 oz or 4 tablespoons) ham
- 1 beaten egg
- 1 tablespoon grated breadcrumbs
- 3 tablespoons oil

Bring the stock to the boil, season it, add tapioca or semolina and cook for 12 to 15 minutes. Pass the veal (or pork) and the ham through a mincer and mix with egg and the breadcrumbs. Shape this mixture into little balls, the size of a grape. Fry them in very hot oil. Put into hot soup and serve.

GERMAN HORSERADISH SOUP

4 Servings

- 1 litre (2 pints or 4 cups) stock
- salt and pepper
- 1 tablespoon freshly grated horseradish

Season stock to taste, bring to the boil. Put horseradish into a soup tureen, pour hot soup over it and serve.

MEXICAN CHICK PEA SOUP

This substantial soup is often served as a main course, accompanied by a dressed green salad.

6 Servings

- 240 grs (8 oz or 1¼ cups) chick-peas
- salt
- 1 beef bone
- 1 ham bone
- 2 litres (2 quarts or 8 cups) water
- 3 medium-size diced potatoes
- 1 crushed clove garlic
- 1 grated onion
- pinch saffron
- 240 grs (8 oz or 1 cup) sliced boiled bacon
- cayenne pepper

Soak the chick peas overnight in enough water to cover, with a tablespoon salt.

Drain, put in a saucepan with beef and ham bones and water. Bring to the boil, simmer for 1½ hours. Add potatoes, garlic, onion and saffron and simmer for 30 minutes. Take the bones out of the soup. Slice bacon and add to soup. Taste for salt, add more if necessary. Season with cayenne pepper and serve piping hot.

HUNGARIAN GOULASH SOUP

6 Servings

- 1 tablespoon butter
- 120 grs (4 oz or ½ cup) shredded bacon
- 240 grs (8 oz or 1½ cups) chopped onion
- 1½ teaspoons paprika
- ½ teaspoon caraway seed
- pinch marjoram
- 1 crushed clove garlic
- 2 litres (4 pints or 8 cups) beef stock
- ½ kg (1 lb or 2 cups) beef, cut in cubes
- 300 grs (10 oz or 2 cups) peeled chopped tomatoes
- salt
- 360 grs (12 oz or 1¾ cups) peeled, diced potatoes
- 30 grs (1 oz or 4 tablespoons) flour
- 180 ml (6 oz or ¾ cup) water
- 3 frankfurter sausages
- lemon juice

In a large pot heat butter, put in bacon and onion and fry until golden. Add paprika, caraway seed, marjoram and garlic. Stir well and cook for 2 minutes. Add stock, beef, tomatoes and salt to taste. Bring to the boil, simmer for 30 minutes.

Add potatoes and cook until they are done. Mix flour with water and stir into the soup. Simmer until soup thickens.

Poach the frankfurter sausages separately in a little water for a few minutes, drain, skin and slice. Add to soup, check seasoning, squeeze into it a dash of lemon juice and serve.

Poultry and Game Soups

COCK-A-LEEKIE SOUP

Cock-a-leekie provides two dishes: a nourishing soup and the boiled fowl, which is served separately.

6–8 Servings

- 1 boiling fowl
- 1 veal knuckle
- 3 litres (3 quarts) water
- 4 leeks
- 3 large potatoes
- salt and pepper
- pinch sugar
- 2 cloves

Put the fowl and the knuckle in water, bring to the boil, skim. Simmer for 1 hour.

Peel leeks and using the white part only cut into rings. Peel and dice potatoes. Add vegetables to soup, season to taste with salt and pepper, add sugar and cloves, continue to simmer for another hour.

ITALIAN WEDDING SOUP

This is a very fine Abruzzi wedding soup. Good strong chicken broth is served with delicate chicken quenelles, cubes or special "bread" made of flour and grated Parmesan cheese, and small dice of Provolone cheese.

12 Servings

- 2 large chickens
- 2 sets chicken giblets
- 1 diced carrot
- 2 sliced leeks
- 1 onion stuck with 2 cloves
- 2 shredded stalks celery
- 5 litres (5 quarts) water
- 1 white of egg for clarifying stock
- 2 lightly beaten eggs
- 12 yolks
- 12 whites of egg
- 60 grs (2 oz or 1¼ cups) freshly grated breadcrumbs
- 75 grs (2½ oz or 10 tablespoons) Parmesan cheese
- salt and pepper
- 90 grs (3 oz or ¾ cup) sifted flour
- 135 grs (4½ oz or ¾ cup) diced Provolone cheese

Cut off the breast fillet from the chickens and reserve for quenelles. Use the rest of the chicken meat, bones, giblets and all the vegetables and water to make good consommé. Clarify with a white of egg (p. 85). Strain, keep cooked chicken meat for some other dish. Remove all fat from consommé.

Skin reserved chicken breasts and mince or chop finely. Combine with beaten eggs, breadcrumbs, 2 tablespoons Parmesan cheese, and salt and pepper to taste. Mix well, shape into small balls and poach in salted boiling water for 15 minutes. Drain well. Turn on oven set to 190°C (375°F or Gas Regulo 4). Beat the yolks. Whisk the whites until stiff and fold into yolks. Little by little stir in flour and remaining Parmesan cheese. Divide mixture between 2 shallow baking tins and bake the Parmesan bread for 30 – 35 minutes. Remove from oven, cool and dice. Reheat consommé, add chicken quenelles, cubes of Parmesan bread and diced Provolone cheese and serve.

CHICKEN NOODLE SOUP

6–8 Servings

- noodle paste (p 154)
- 1 boiling fowl
- 2½ litres (5 pints or 10 cups) water
- salt and pepper
- 1–2 medium-sized onions, quartered
- 3 stalks celery, shredded
- 1 peeled quartered parsnip
- 2 peeled quartered carrots
- 1 tablespoon chopped dill or parsley

Roll out the paste on a floured board into very thin sheets and leave on a cloth to dry for an hour. Fold the dough lightly and with a sharp knife cut into strips. Shake the noodles lightly to separate them and leave on a cloth to dry until hard.

Home-made noodles can be made in advance and stored in airtight jars.

Wash the chicken thoroughly, joint and chop carcass into pieces. Wash all giblets, scald and peel gizzard. Put chicken, giblets and carcass into a saucepan with water, bring to the boil, skim until the surface is clear.

Season, add vegetables, cover and simmer on low heat for 2½–3 hours. Strain, leave until cold then remove surface fat. Bring the soup to the boil, add noodles, cook for 10 minutes.

Sprinkle with chopped dill and serve.

The chicken and the vegetables used for making the broth can be used for croquettes.

CHICKEN SOUP WITH KREPLACH

Prepare broth as described in recipe for Chicken Noodle Soup (p. 46) instead of noodles. Finish cooking and garnish as described.

ITALIAN SOUP WITH NOODLES AND CHICKEN LIVERS

4 Servings

100 grs (3½ oz or ⅞ cup) fine noodles
240 grs (8 oz or 1½ cups) tender young peas, shelled
salt
water
1 litre (2 pints or 4 cups) chicken stock
240 grs (8 oz or 1 cup) sliced chicken livers
1½ tablespoons butter
grated Parmesan cheese
pepper

This is a delicious soup, easy and quick to make, but you must have all ingredients ready and perform three simple operations simultaneously.

Cook noodles and peas separately in salted boiling water for 5–6 minutes and drain.

While the noodles are cooking, bring stock to the boil and fry chicken livers in butter. Season to taste with salt and pepper.

Combine stock with noodles, peas, chicken livers and their buttery pan juices. Reheat to boiling point and serve with a sprinkling of Parmesan cheese.

CAPPELLETTI IN BRODO

6 Servings

1 chicken breast
2 tablespoons butter
480 grs (1 lb or 2 cups) cottage cheese
1 egg
1 egg yolk
salt and pepper
¼ teaspoon nutmeg
ravioli paste (p 144)
4 litres (4 quarts) boiling salted water
1½ litres (1½ quarts or 6 cups) light consommé (p 85)
grated Parmesan cheese

Fry chicken in butter to brown evenly on both sides. Chop or mince finely. Put in a bowl, add cottage cheese, egg and yolk. Season with salt, pepper and nutmeg. Mix well, to make smooth filling. Roll out paste into paper-thin sheets on lightly floured board. Cut into little circles. Put a teaspoon of filling in the middle of each circle, fold over and shape into little 'hats'. Press to seal the edges firmly.

Drop cappelletti a few at a time into boiling water, boil fast for 6–7 minutes or until tender.

Bring consommé to the boil. Drain cappelletti, add to consommé and serve. Hand grated cheese for sprinkling on soup.

ITALIAN NOODLE SOUP WITH PESTO

4 Servings

- 1 litre (1 quart or 4 cups) chicken stock
- 120 grs (4 oz or 1 cup) small pasta (stars, alphabet, etc)
- salt and pepper
- 1–2 tablespoons pesto (p 23)

Bring the stock to the boil, cook pasta until done, but *al dente,* that is, still giving a pleasant resistance to the teeth. Season to taste with salt and pepper, add pesto, stir and serve.

YEMENI CHICKEN AND MARROW SOUP

6 Servings

- 1 jointed chicken
- 1½ litres (1½ quarts) water
- ½ kg (1 lb) young marrows
- 2 medium-sized tomatoes
- 4–5 spring onions
- salt
- pinch hawayij (see p 150)

Put the chicken in a pan of water, bring to the boil, skim off all the scum which rises to the surface until the liquid is clear. Cover and simmer for 1 hour. Wash and dry the marrow. If young, leave unpeeled, cut in half and then slice. If the marrow is past its prime, peel and remove seeds.

Drop tomatoes into boiling water for a few seconds to loosen skins. Peel and slice tomatoes. Add marrows and tomatoes to soup. Continue to simmer for 20 minutes. Chop spring onions. Add to soup. Season to taste with salt and hawayij and serve piping hot.

TURKISH CHICKEN SOUP

6 Servings

- 2½ litres (2½ quarts) chicken stock
- 120 grs (4 oz or 1⅓ cups) fine vermicelli
- salt
- 1½ tablespoons cornflour
- 3 tablespoons milk
- 2 raw yolks
- 1½ tablespoons lemon juice
- 2–3 tablespoons butter
- 1½ teaspoons paprika

Cook vermicelli in stock for 10–12 minutes. Season to taste.

Dilute cornflour with milk, blend into the soup and simmer for a few minutes, until the soup begins to thicken. Remove from heat. Put soup bowls to heat. Mix yolks with lemon juice and little by little incorporate in the soup. Keep hot, but on no account allow to boil. Melt butter, work paprika into it and cook together to amalgamate, to make a dressing.

Pour soup into individual bowls, float a spoonful of butter and paprika dressing over each and serve.

ARMENIAN SOUP WITH YOGHURT AND MINT

6 Servings

- 1 litre (1 quart or 4 cups) stock or consommé
- 2½ dcl (½ pint or 1 cup) plain yoghurt
- 2–3 tablespoons butter
- 2 tablespoons flour
- salt and pepper
- chopped fresh mint

Bring stock to the boil. Little by little blend in yoghurt.

Separately, in a large pan, heat butter, stir in flour and cook a blond roux, i.e. without allowing the mixture of flour and butter to brown. Dilute with yoghurt flavoured stock, blending it in a little at a time. As soon as the soup comes to the boil, remove from heat, garnish with mint and serve.

CANADIAN PEANUT SOUP

6 Servings

- 1 finely chopped onion
- 2 tablespoons butter
- 1 litre (2 pints or 4 cups) chicken stock
- 120 grs (4 oz or ½ cup) peanut butter
- 120 mls (4 oz or ½ cup) cream
- salt and pepper
- 60 grs (2 oz or ½ cup) roasted peanuts

In a saucepan fry the onion in butter until soft and transparent. Add stock, bring to the boil, simmer for 10 minutes.

Blend peanut butter with cream and stir the mixture into the soup, keeping the pan on lowest possible heat. Season to taste, reheat without allowing the soup to boil, garnish with roasted peanuts and serve.

BRAZILIAN CHICKEN AND RICE SOUP

6 Servings

- 1 boiling fowl
- 3 litres (3 quarts) water
- 1 chopped onion
- 1 chopped carrot
- 3 sprigs parsley
- 2 tablespoons chopped chives
- salt and pepper
- 2 tablespoons chopped mint
- 2 tablespoons chopped parsley
- 120 grs (4 oz or 9 tablespoons rice

Bring the chicken to the boil in water, skim, simmer for 30 minutes. Add onion, carrot, sprigs of parsley and chives. Season to taste. Simmer until the chicken is tender. Remove chicken from soup. Put mint and parsley into soup. Wash rice and add to soup. Bring to the boil, simmer until rice is tender. Take chicken meat off the bones, dice and drop into soup. Check seasoning and serve.

WATERZOOTJE

Waterzootje really is a Flemish version of cotriade or bouillabaisse, a substantial fish soup, but whereas in France the dish is cooked with oil, in Belgium and Holland butter is used.

Here is a chicken waterzootje.

6–8 Servings

1 boiling fowl
lemon
3 litres (3 quarts) chicken stock or water
2 small onions each stuck with 2 cloves
3 shredded leeks, white part only
2 shredded stalks celery
2 tablespoons butter
bouquet garni
salt and pepper
60 ml (2 oz or 4 tablespoons) dry white wine
chopped parsley

Rub the chicken with cut lemon to tenderise. Bring to the boil in stock, skim off scum which rises to the surface. Add onions. Lightly fry leeks and celery in butter, add to stock, together with bouquet garni. Bring to the boil, season to taste, add wine and simmer until the chicken is tender.

Remove bouquet garni and onions studded with cloves. Take the chicken out of the pot, cut into portions, put back in the soup to reheat and serve garnished with chopped parsley.

CAUCASIAN CHIKHIRTMA

6–8 Servings

1 chicken
2 litres (4 pints or 8 cups) water
2 chopped onions
2 tablespoons butter
1 tablespoon flour
½ teaspoon saffron
2 tablespoons wine vinegar
2 raw yolks
1 teaspoon salt
½ teaspoon freshly ground black pepper
2 tablespoons chopped dill or parsley

Wash, dry and cut chicken up into smallish pieces, allowing 3–4 pieces to be served per person in the soup plate. Bring to the boil in water, skim surface, simmer until tender. Remove chicken and strain soup. Lightly fry onion in butter until soft. Stir in flour, cook together without browning for 2–3 minutes. Dilute with a cup of stock, blending in a little at a time.

Pour strained stock back into the saucepan, add fried onion sauce, saffron, salt and pepper. Bring to the boil.

Separately bring vinegar to the boil and add to soup. Stir, add chicken and bring to the boil once more. Remove from heat.

Beat yolks in a bowl with a ladleful of cooled stock, stir into soup, reheat without allowing it to boil, sprinkle with dill and serve.

SOTO AJAM (SINGAPORE CHICKEN SOUP WITH VERMICELLI)

6 Servings

- 1 boiling fowl
- 1 teaspoon turmeric
- 2½ cm (1 inch) piece of green ginger
- 2–3 cloves garlic
- 1 onion
- salt
- 1–2 tablespoons peanut oil
- 120 grs (2 ozs ⅔ cup) Chinese vermicelli
- 10–12 spring onions
- 6 slices lime

Simmer the chicken in salted water to cover until tender. Drain and bone the chicken, leaving the stock meanwhile to boil down by half, to concentrate it. Drop the bones back into the stock as you take the chicken meat off them. Cut chicken into strips. Pound the turmeric, ginger, garlic and onion, with a pinch of salt in a mortar, or reduce to paste in a blender. Fry the mixture in oil for 3 minutes, stirring constantly.

Strain the stock, add chicken, stir in spice paste, bring to the boil, simmer for 10 minutes uncovered. Add vermicelli and boil fast for 5 minutes. Check seasoning and add salt, if necessary. Chop spring onions, sprinkle into the pan, cook for 5 minutes. Serve the broth with chicken and vermicelli in individual bowls. Put a slice of lime in each bowl before serving. If limes are not available, use lemon.

HUNGARIAN GIBLET SOUP

4 Servings

- 1 small chopped onion
- 2 sets giblets, cleaned and chopped
- 1 diced carrot
- small piece diced parsnip
- 2 peeled sliced tomatoes
- 2 tablespoons chicken fat or butter
- 1 tablespoon flour
- 1 litre (1 quart) water or chicken bone stock
- salt and pepper

Brown the giblets, except the liver, and the vegetables in chicken fat over low heat for 10–12 minutes. Dust with flour, blend it in and cook gently for 2–3 minutes. Gradually dilute with stock, bring to the boil, then simmer until the giblets are tender. 2–3 minutes before the end of cooking add liver. Season to taste and serve.

CHICKEN CHOWDER

6 Servings

- 1 chicken 2 kgs (4 lb)
- 120 grs (4 oz or 9 tablespoons) rice
- 2 litres (2 quarts) water
- little oil
- 30 grs (1 oz) rice noodles
- 15 grs (½ oz) fresh ginger
- 30 grs (1 oz) preserved parsnips
- 1 tablespoon sesame oil
- soya sauce
- salt and pepper
- 6 chopped spring onions

Clean the chicken and together with the rice, place in a saucepan, cover with water and cook for 2½ hours. Heat some oil in a saucepan, put in noodles, cook for a few seconds and remove from heat. Remove chicken, bone it and cut meat into fine slices.

Slice ginger and parsnips. Add chicken, ginger and parsnips to the chowder and cook for 3 minutes.

Decant the chowder into small individual bowls, sprinkle into each a few drops of sesame oil and soya sauce, a little salt and pepper, and a few drops of the oil in which the noodles were cooked.

Stir, garnish each bowl with spring onions and rice noodles.

Variations: Duck chowder – clean the duck and proceed as described in the recipe for Chicken Chowder.

MINCED CHICKEN AND CORN CHOWDER WITH ALMONDS

4–6 Servings

- 1 can sweet corn (cream style)
- 1 teaspoon cornflour
- 2 tablespoons cold water
- 2 teaspoons salt
- ½ teaspoon pepper
- 1½–2 litres (1½–2 quarts) hot chicken stock
- 360 grs (12 oz or 1½ cups) uncooked breast of chicken, minced
- 2 egg whites, beaten
- 2 tablespoons roasted almonds, chopped

Mince the corn, to break up the kernels.

Blend cornflour with water, add to corn, season with salt and pepper and stir into the stock.

Pound the chicken until smooth and add egg whites. Add to corn soup. Bring to the boil again, then simmer very gently for 8–10 minutes. Sprinkle with almonds and serve.

SWEET CORN SOUP WITH CHICKEN

4 Servings

- 250 grs (8 oz or 1 cup) breast of chicken (keep 1–2 slices finely shredded for garnish)
- 1 small knob ginger
- 1 can sweet corn
- ½ teaspoon Ve-Tsin
- 1 teaspoon Shao Shing (or dry sherry)
- cornflour (for dredging)
- 1 egg, well beaten
- salt
- little ham, finely shredded
- 1 teaspoon cornflour (for thickening)
- 2 tablespoons cold water

Slice half the chicken finely and bring to the boil in 1½ litres (1½ quarts) water together with the bones and ginger. Simmer for 30 minutes, then add sweet corn, Ve-Tsin and Shao Shing.

Simmer for 5 minutes, add rest of chicken finely shredded and dredged with dry cornflour.

Add egg, stir, season to taste. Garnish with ham and chicken and thicken with cornflour mixed with water.

CHINESE CHICKEN SOUP WITH STUFFED MUSHROOMS

6 Servings

- 18–24 large cap mushrooms
- 180 grs (6 oz or ¾ cup) peeled chopped prawns
- 240 grs (8 oz or 1 cup) uncooked minced pork
- 1 teaspoon chopped onion
- 3 finely chopped water chestnuts
- 1 teaspoon soya sauce
- pinch salt
- 1 tablespoon cornflour
- 1½ litres (3 pints or 6 cups) chicken stock

Remove stems from mushrooms, wash and leave gill side down to drain. Dry on a cloth.

Mix prawns, pork, onion, water chestnuts and soya sauce. Season with salt, add 1 tablespoon stock and cornflour. Knead the mixture to amalgamate. Taking equal portions, roll into small balls and pack one of these into each mushroom cap. Put in a steamer, stuffed side up, cover tightly and steam for 15–20 minutes.

Heat the stock, float the stuffed mushrooms on top and serve.

CHICKEN AND MUSHROOM SOUP

6 Servings

- 60 grs (2 oz or 4 tablespoons) chicken breast
- 1 teaspoon cornflour
- 2 tablespoons cold water
- 60 grs (2 oz or 1 cup) mushrooms
- 60 grs (2 oz or 4 tablespoons) bamboo shoots
- 1½ litres (1½ quarts) hot chicken stock
- 1 dessertspoon light soya sauce
- ½ teaspoon salt
- few spring onions, chopped

Shred chicken and mix with cornflour and water. Slice mushrooms and bamboo shoots, cook for 5 minutes in stock. Add chicken and simmer until it turns white. Add soya sauce, salt and spring onions before serving.

CHINESE CHICKEN SOUP WITH EGG

4 Servings

- 2½–3 tablespoons cornflour
- 2½–3 tablespoons cold water
- ½ teaspoon sugar
- 1 teaspoon salt
- ¼ teaspoon pepper
- 1½ litres (1½ quarts) hot chicken stock
- 2 eggs, beaten
- 2–3 spring onions, chopped

Make a smooth paste of cornflour and water, sugar, salt and pepper. Pour into the stock and stir. Bring to the boil, reduce heat, add eggs, stir for 1 minute until the eggs go into shreds. Remove from heat, garnish with spring onions and serve.

SOUP WITH CHICKEN AND FRIED NOODLES

6 Servings

- 180 grs (6 oz or ¾ cup) breast of chicken
- 30 grs (1 oz or ½ cup) mushrooms
- 30 grs (1 oz or 2 tablespoons) bambo shoots
- 1 round fried noodles
- boiling water
- salt and pepper
- hot chicken stock
- little sesame oil
- 30 grs (1 oz or 3 tablespoons) spring onions, chopped

Slice chicken, mushrooms and bamboo shoots finely. Place noodles in pan of boiling water for 2 minutes, then drain and put in serving bowl. Keep warm. Place chicken, mushrooms and bamboo shoots in a pan. Add double the amount of stock required to cover the ingredients, and cook for 3 minutes. Add salt and pepper to taste and pour over the noodles.

Sprinkle with a few drops of sesame oil and the spring onions and serve.

CANTONESE CHICKEN AND HAM SOUP

6 Servings

- 1 boiling fowl
- 2 litres (2 quarts) water
- 60 grs (2 oz or ½ cup) awabi, sliced
- 2 tablespoons Shao Shing or dry sherry
- 2 teaspoons salt
- 125 grs (4 oz or ½ cup) Chinese ham, shredded
- few spring onions chopped

Put chicken in water and bring to the boil. Add awabi, Shao Shing, salt and ham.

Simmer gently for 2½–3 hours. Before serving, sprinkle with spring onions.

Note : If awabi is not available, prawns can be substituted.

TORI-NO-MIZUDAKI (JAPANESE CHICKEN SOUP)

4 Servings

- 1 jointed chicken
- 2½ litres (2½ quarts) water
- 1–2 sliced leeks
- 1 tablespoon salt
- juice of 1 lemon
- 4–5 tablespoons shoyu

Bone the chicken joints, put meat and bones in a pan of water, bring to the boil, skim, simmer until meat is tender then carefully remove all bones. Cut meat into large dice, add leeks, put back in the pan and reheat.

Mix salt, lemon juice and shoyu and stir the mixture into the soup. Simmer for a few minutes, just long enough for the leeks to cook through, and serve in individual covered bowls.

Note: In Japan, bitter orange juice is often used instead of lemon juice for this soup and a small dish of very fine dry salt is served at the same time. The guests dip pieces of chicken into it if they want more seasoning.

DUCK AND ORANGE PEEL SOUP

6 Servings

- 1 duck 2 kg (4 lb)
- little oil
- 30 grs (1 oz) dried orange peel
- 2 litres (2 quarts) hot chicken stock
- salt

Open duck down centre back and remove inside and backbone. Heat oil in pan and brown duck quickly on all sides. Place in a dish, cut side up.

Soak orange peel in cold water for 20 minutes and scrape out pith. Toss peel in a little oil for a couple of minutes. Put peel in duck and moisten with enough stock to fill duck three-quarters full. Add salt to taste.

Put dish in pan of water and steam until duck is tender. Take out orange peel and remaining bones of duck. Serve duck in the soup.

CHINESE PIGEON SOUP

6 Servings

- 2 young pigeons, cleaned
- 6 dried Chinese mushrooms
- 1 teaspoon brandy
- $1\frac{1}{2}$ litres ($1\frac{1}{2}$ quarts) water
- salt and pepper
- $\frac{1}{2}$ tablespoon light soya sauce

Cut pigeons into quarters.

Soak mushrooms in hot water and remove stalks. Place all ingredients in double saucepan, bring to boil, season to taste and steam until pigeons are tender. Serve with soya sauce.

CHICKEN STUFFED WITH SHARK'S FINS, IN SOUP

6 Servings

- 250 grs (8 oz) shark's fins
- 1 small piece fresh ginger
- salt
- 1 clove garlic, crushed
- water
- 1 chicken leg
- 60 grs (2 oz or 4 tablespoons) Chinese ham (or other smoked ham)
- 60 grs (2 oz or 4 tablespoons) bamboo shoots
- 1 young chicken 2 kg (4 lb)
- 3 teaspoons Shao Shing wine (p 157)
- chicken stock

Soak the shark's fins in water for 24 hours. Boil them slowly for 4 hours, with ginger, salt and garlic in double the amount of fresh water required to cover them. Drain and remove any flesh on the fins. Put it in a basin, place the chicken leg on top and steam slowly for 2 hours. Remove the chicken leg and any water which may have dropped on the fins.

Cut Chinese ham and bamboo shoots into fine strips. Clean chicken, open the neck and take out the inside and all the bones, taking care not to break the skin. Sprinkle with Shao Shing on the inside.

Place shark's fins, bamboo shoots and Chinese ham in the chicken together with enough stock to fill the chicken. Sew up hole at neck.

Place chicken in a pan with enough stock to cover. Steam for 1 hour, remove 'stitches' and serve.

LOTUS SEED AND DUCK SOUP, HONG KONG STYLE

6–8 Servings

- 1 duck (about 1–$1\frac{1}{2}$ kg or $2\frac{1}{2}$ lb)
- 2 litres (2 quarts) water
- 60 grs (2 oz or 4 tablespoons) bamboo shoots
- 60 grs (2 oz or 1 cup) fresh mushrooms
- 30 grs (1 oz or 2 tablespoons) water chestnuts

1 teaspoon cornflour
1 dessertspoon Shao Shing or dry sherry
1 can lotus seeds
1 teaspoon sesame oil
1 teaspoon soya sauce
salt and pepper

Bone duck and boil the bones in water for 2 hours. Slice duck meat finely.

Shred bamboo shoots, mushrooms and water chestnuts and mix together.

Dilute cornflour with 1 dcl ($\frac{1}{4}$ pint or $\frac{1}{2}$ cup) water, add Shao Shing and pour over duck. Remove bones from soup, then add water chestnuts, bamboo shoots, mushrooms, lotus seed and duck meat. Cook for 3 minutes, add sesame oil and soya sauce. Season with salt and pepper and serve.

BIRDS' NEST SOUP

6 Servings

125 grs (4 oz) birds' nest
2 litres (2 quarts) chicken stock
1 leg of chicken
2 teaspoons water chestnut flour
1–2 tablespoons water
salt and pepper
1 egg white
60 grs (2 oz or 4 tablespoons) cooked chicken, chopped
30 grs (1 oz or 2 tablespoons) ham, finely chopped
60 grs (2 oz or $\frac{1}{2}$ cup) fresh mushrooms, chopped
few spring onions, chopped

Soak the birds' nest in hot water for 4 hours. Simmer in chicken stock for 10 minutes. Transfer to fireproof dish, place chicken leg on top and steam for 2 hours. Remove chicken leg and any water that may have dropped on the birds' nest.

Mix water chestnut flour with water to a smooth paste. Place birds' nest in saucepan, cover with stock, bring to boil, season with salt and pepper and stir in water chestnut paste.

Simmer for 2 minutes, stirring all the time. Add white of egg, and when soup becomes semi-transparent, garnish with chicken, ham, mushrooms and spring onions. Serve.

CATALAN CHRISTMAS SOUP

6–8 Servings

8–10 slices of bread
3–4 tablespoons goose, turkey or chicken fat
giblets, cooked and chopped
2 litres (2 quarts) stock
salt and pepper

Fry some slices of bread lightly in the fat left over from roast turkey, goose or chicken. (The amount of bread can be varied.) Put the fried bread and the giblets into a saucepan. Pour in the stock, season and simmer for 20 minutes. Put in the oven for a few minutes before serving.

STRACCIATELLA

6 Servings

- 2 litres (2 quarts) hot chicken stock or consommé
- 3 eggs
- 4 tablespoons grated Parmesan cheese
- 2 tablespoons fine semolina
- salt and pepper
- pinch grated nutmeg

Beat the eggs with cheese and semolina, season to taste with salt, pepper and nutmeg, then dilute with a cupful of stock. Stir well. Bring stock to the boil, remove from heat, add beaten egg mixture, put back to heat, simmer for 3–4 minutes, whisking constantly. Do not allow the soup to boil after adding the eggs. Serve at once.

ZUPPA PAVESE

6 Servings

- 2 litres (2 quarts) hot chicken consommé
- small slices of white bread (2–3 per portion)
- butter
- 6 eggs
- grated Parmesan cheese

Put the consommé to heat. Fry the slices of bread in butter and lightly poach the eggs in consommé. As soon as done, remove eggs with a slotted spoon, trim and put one in each individual heated plate or bowl. Pour hot consommé on the eggs, float pieces of fried bread on the soup, sprinkle them with cheese and serve at once.

MALAYSIAN CHICKEN SOUP

6–8 Servings

- 1 jointed chicken
- 2 litres (4 pints or 8 cups) water
- 1 tablespoon salt
- 2 medium-sized onions
- 1 teaspoon fresh ginger
- 1 tablespoon soya sauce
- 3 tablespoons peanut oil
- 1 cup raw rice
- pinch chilli powder
- pinch Ve-Tsin

For garnish:

- 2–3 hard boiled eggs

Put the chicken in a pan with water, bring to the boil and skim until no more scum rises to the surface. Quarter 1 onion and add to soup with ginger. Simmer for 1–1¼ hours, or until the chicken is tender. Strain the stock. Bone the chicken, shred it, and sprinkle with soya sauce. Cut the remaining onion into thin slices. Fry in half the oil, until pale golden. Remove, drain well and keep hot. Add remaining oil, and gently fry the rice until transparent, stirring all the time.

Bring stock to the boil. Add rice, chilli and Ve-Tsin. Simmer gently for 18–20 minutes, by which time the rice should be tender. Add chicken, check seasoning, add more salt and chilli if needed. Re-heat and serve with a topping of fried onions and slices of hard-boiled eggs.

Fish Soups

BOUILLABAISSE

This is one of the greatest and most delicious of fish soups. For a truly authentic bouillabaisse one vital ingredient is available only in the Mediterranean. This is rascasse, a fish which is not very good for eating but gives an exquisite flavour to bouillabaisse. Bouillabaisse needs careful timing. The amount of ingredients given below should not be cooked for longer than 15 minutes. It is essential to keep up the very fast boiling, as described in the recipe which follows, to enable the water and oil to emulsify and give the bouillabaisse its smooth consistency.

6–8 Servings

- 250 grs (½ lb) turbot
- 250 grs (1 lb) rock salmon
- 250 grs (½ lb) conger eel
- 2 dozen Dublin Bay prawns
- 250 grs (½ lb) whiting
- 250 grs (½ lb) bass
- 250–375 grs (½–¾ lb) red mullet
- 4 pounded cloves garlic
- 2 chopped onions
- shredded white of 2 leeks
- 250 grs (1 lb or 1 cup) peeled, sliced tomatoes
- pinch thyme
- ½ bay leaf
- 2 tablespoons roughly chopped parsley
- 1 tablespoon chopped fennel
- a piece of orange peel
- 1 dcl (1 gill or ½ cup) olive oil
- boiling water
- salt and pepper
- ½ teaspoon saffron
- 6–8 slices bread

Clean the fish, bone and cut into uniform pieces; halve the prawns lengthwise. Put garlic, onions, leeks, tomatoes, thyme, bay leaf, 1 tablespoon parsley, fennel, and orange peel into a saucepan. Place the firm-fleshed fish (turbot, rock salmon, eel) and the prawns on top of this vegetable foundation. Pour oil over the whole. From this moment, for a successful bouillabaisse, timing is vital. Do not proceed further if you are not going to be ready to serve it within a quarter of an hour. If you are ready to go on, heat to boiling point, pour over enough boiling water just to cover the ingredients and boil very fast for 7 minutes, adding salt, pepper and saffron. Add the rest of the fish – the more delicate whiting, bass and mullet (which would disintegrate if put in to cook earlier), and continue to boil very fast for another 7 minutes. Put a piece of bread, home-made if possible, (do not use toast) into each deep soup plate (or into a soup tureen), pour the liquid on it and serve at once. Arrange the fish and the prawns on a separate platter, sprinkle with chopped parsley and serve at the same time.

COTRIADE

This is a Breton version of bouillabaisse and the greater the variety of fresh fish used, the better the cotriade. Hake, cod, sea bass, mackerel, John Dory, gurnet, red mullet and fresh sardines are all good for this dish. One or two large fish heads greatly improve the stock.

4–6 Servings

- 1½ litres (1½ quarts or 5 cups) good fish stock (page 21)
- 3–4 tablespoons butter
- 2 large sliced onions
- 3–4 large sliced potatoes
- bouquet garni
- 1 kg (2 lb) assorted firm fish
- salt and pepper
- 8–12 slices French bread
- 1–2 cloves garlic

Use the fish heads, bones and trimmings for the fish stock. Heat butter in a saucepan and fry onions until pale golden. Add stock, bring to the boil, add potatoes and bouquet garni. Simmer for 15 minutes.

Cut fish into portions, add to soup, season to taste with salt and pepper, boil rapidly for 10 minutes.

Dry the bread slices in the oven, rub with cut garlic and put these croûtons into a heated soup tureen.

Carefully remove fish portions onto a heated serving dish. Garnish with vegetables from the stock pot in which the fish was cooked. Pour soup over croûtons. Serve soup in tureen and fish with the vegetables in its serving dish at the same time.

ZUPPA DI PESCE / ITALIAN FISH SOUP

8 Servings

- 2½–3 kg (5–6 lbs) mixed fish (cod, haddock, mullet, eel, carp, mackerel, whiting)
- 2–3 small squid
- 100 ml (3½ oz or 7 tablespoons) olive oil

30 grs (1 oz or 2 tablespoons) butter
2 medium sized, thinly sliced onions
1–2 crushed cloves garlic
1 kg (2 lb or 6 cups) peeled chopped tomatoes
2–3 tablespoons chopped parsley
1 tablespoon tomato paste
boiling water, fish stock (p 21) and/or
180 ml (6 oz or $\frac{3}{4}$ cup) dry white wine
2 tablespoons vinegar
salt and pepper

A good Italian fish soup requires a variety of fish, it is best to plan it therefore for 8–10 people.

Wash and cut the fish into portions. Use heads and trimmings to make fish stock and strain. It will not be very strong, but will certainly have more body and flavour than plain water.

While the fish stock is cooking, prepare the sauce which makes the foundation of the zuppa di pesce.

Heat oil and butter in a big saucepan. Fry onion until it becomes soft. Add garlic, cook together for 2–3 minutes. Add tomatoes and parsley and simmer for 5 minutes, stirring from time to time. Dilute tomato paste with a cupful of the fish stock and pour into saucepan. Simmer uncovered for 20 minutes. Put in fish, add remaining fish stock. You must have enough liquid to cover the fish. If there is not enough fish stock, make up with boiling water. Bring to the boil, add wine and vinegar, simmer gently for 15 minutes. Season with salt and freshly ground pepper.

PORTUGUESE FISH SOUP

This is one of those substantial soups to be served as a main course.

6 Servings
1 medium-sized onion
2–3 tablespoons olive oil
375 grs (12 oz) cod or haddock
$1\frac{1}{2}$ litres (3 pints or 6 cups) water
180 grs (6 oz or $\frac{1}{4}$ cup) peeled prawns
3 tablespoons chopped parsley
salt and pepper
1 teaspoon chopped basil
3 hard-boiled eggs
6 slices toast
2 tablespoons roasted silvered almonds

Chop the onions finely and fry lightly in oil, using a saucepan large enough to take all ingredients. Cut fish into portions and lay on top of onions. Add water, prawns and parsley. Bring to the boil, season to taste and add basil. Cover and simmer for 8–10 minutes. Chop the hard-boiled eggs. Put some hard-boiled egg and a slice of toasted bread in each plate, pour soup over them, sprinkle with almonds and serve piping hot.

COSTA BRAVA SOUP

6 Servings

- 300 grs (10 oz) monk-fish
- 300 grs (10 oz) hake
- $1\frac{3}{4}$ litres ($1\frac{3}{4}$ quarts) water
- 1 sliced onion
- 2 teaspoons salt
- 240 grs (1 lb) tomatoes
- 60 grs (2 oz or 6 tablespoons) potato flour
- 3 raw egg yolks
- 2 tablespoons milk
- 60 grs (2 oz or 4 tablespoons) butter

Wash the fish but do not cut. Put in a pan with water, onion and salt. Bring to the boil. Drop in tomatoes and let them cook until soft. Remove tomatoes with a perforated spoon, then rub through a sieve into the pan with the fish soup. Cook for 30 minutes. Remove fish and strain soup. In a clean saucepan, mix potato flour with a cupful of cooked fish stock. Gradually add the rest of the fish stock, stirring. Mash hake, add to soup and simmer for 15 minutes, stirring frequently. Dice the monk-fish.

Dilute yolks with milk in a soup tureen. Blend in butter, adding it in small pieces. Put in diced monk-fish. Pour in hot soup, stir and serve.

UKHA

Ukha originally started in Russia as a simple fish soup, a strictly lenten dish. It did not take long to develop into a luxurious soup, robbing Lent of all austerity. In an 1861 edition of a best-selling cookery book by a formidable lady called Yelena Molokhovets, a light chicken stock, Lent not withstanding is advocated for fresh salmon ukha, to make it 'fit for an archbishop'. Perhaps in gratitude for such consideration to the clergy, 50 years later, to mark the appearance of the 28th edition of the 4,000-recipe volume, among the letters printed as an introduction to the book, there was a fulsome tribute from an archbishop. He said that her book had proved to be 'a veritable talisman, safeguarding the sanctity of marriage'. Husbands of women who used her book were so delighted with the food served to them at home that they could easily resist the lure of restaurants and suchlike places 'with their temptations which undermine the family'.

I have a thing about Madame Molokhovets and read her as a historical social document. For instance, she says that when geese, ducks, etc., are slaughtered before some great gorging festival, the feathers should not be thrown away. 'Keep them in sacks. Then on dark winter evenings, the servant girls can strip the down off the feathers for pillows.'

A good court-bouillon (p. 20), strengthened with fumet (p. 21) is essential for ukha and you need an assortment of fish to give it taste, strength, sweetness and a certain interesting viscosity. Perch and bass are recommended for their flavour and gelatinous qualities, ling and allied fish for sweetness and delicacy.

Small perch used for fish stock only need to be washed and gutted; the scales need not be scraped off as they add to the texture. Perch and any heads used for stock should be boiled until they disintegrate completely, then strained through muslin.

To give fish soup perfect translucency Russian cooks, to this day, clarify it with fresh caviar! Sounds like unbelievable waste, but this is how they do it: pound 60 grs (2 oz) caviar – pressed or soft – in a mortar, gradually adding 3–4 tablespoons of cold water. Dilute with a cupful of hot strained fish stock – this constitutes the clarifying agent. The mixture is added to boiling, strained fish stock in two goes, allowing it to come to the boil in between. Simmer for 5 minutes, remove from heat, allow to stand for 15 minutes for the caviar to subside, then strain. To come back to earth, 2 egg whites do the job of 60 grs (2 oz) of caviar and cost much less!

For a special occasion serve ukha with a fish coulibiac (p. 138).

SALMON AND CHAMPAGNE UKHA

(See introductory note on ukha)

4 Servings

1 litre (1 quart or 4 cups) stock
2 egg whites
1 tablespoon chopped tarragon and chervil
salt and pepper
½ kg (1 lb) salmon, cut into portions
1½ tablespoons chopped dill or spring onions
½ bottle champagne
1 peeled thinly sliced lemon

Slightly warm the stock, preferably good court-bouillon for fish (p. 20) strengthened with fumet (p. 21), or a light chicken stock. The stock should be barely tepid.

Put egg whites in a pan, add tarragon and chervil and whisk to mix. Pour on stock and bring to the boil, whisking all the time. As soon as boiling is established, turn down heat and simmer very gently for 30 minutes. Season to taste. Strain through napkin rinsed out in water and thoroughly wrung out.

20 minutes before serving, bring stock to the boil, put in salmon portions and poach on simmering heat for 15 minutes. Carefully take out the fish, put in a heated soup tureen, sprinkle with chopped dill or spring onions and keep warm.

In a separate saucepan, heat champagne to boiling point and add to soup. Pour soup over salmon and serve at once. Put 1 lemon slice in each plate. Any dry white wine may be substituted for champagne. Ukha served with fish coulibiac or pirozhki (p. 134) makes a splendid main course.

RUSSIAN WHITEBAIT SOUP

6 Servings

- 480 grs (1 lb) whitebait
- 1½ litres (1½ quarts) vegetable court-bouillon (p 20)
- 90 grs (3 oz or ½ cup) buckwheat (kasha)
- 1½ tablespoons butter
- salt and pepper
- 1 tablespoon lemon juice
- 120 ml (4 oz or ½ cup) cream

Wash the whitebait and remove heads if you object to them. Drain, sprinkle with one teaspoon of salt, and leave in a colander for 30 minutes.

Strain court-bouillon, bring to the boil and add buckwheat. Add butter, stir and simmer until buckwheat is soft. Put in whitebait, boil, remove scum off the top, simmer for 1 minute, add lemon juice, season to taste with salt and freshly ground pepper and remove from heat. Add cream and serve.

CANARY ISLANDS FISH SOUP

6 Servings

- butter or oil
- 1 onion
- 480 grs (1 lb) hake
- 480 grs (1 lb) other fish (cod, haddock)
- 1 litre (2 pints or 4 cups) well scrubbed mussels
- 1½ litres (1½ quarts) water
- 10–12 slices bread
- salt and pepper

Melt 2 tablespoons of butter in a saucepan. Chop the onion, cut the fish into biggish portions, leaving the bones in for the time being, fry lightly with the onion, turning the fish carefully so as not to break it. Take off the fire while you heat some oil in another saucepan and drop in the washed mussels to loosen their shells. Carefully bone the fish and replace in the saucepan, add mussels and their oil. Pour in water. Cook for a few minutes while you prepare a few pieces of fried bread (the quantity will depend on how thick you want the soup – say a couple of pieces per person). Season well – 2–3 teaspoons of salt and a generous pinch of pepper – then float the fried bread on top, simmer for half an hour and serve.

SPANISH LENT SOUP

6 Servings

- 2 carrots
- 2 leeks
- 3 tomatoes
- 2 sprigs parsley
- butter
- several heads of hake (or pieces of any other fish)
- 2 litres (2 quarts) water
- ½ litre (1 pint or 2 cups) mussels
- 1 tablespoon oil
- 6 tablespoons rice
- 3 fillets of sole (or plaice)
- salt and pepper

Clean, peel and slice the carrots, the leeks and the tomatoes and chop the parsley, fry lightly in 2 tablespoons of butter in a saucepan. Add the heads of hake and all other fish except the sole. Brown very lightly and add water. Cook for 90 minutes, strain. Wash the mussels. Heat oil, drop the mussels in, loosen and discard the mussel shells and add to the soup. Wash the rice in several waters and put in the soup. Cook for 15 minutes. Wash the sole fillets, cut them in half longways and add to the soup. Season well, Simmer for 10 minutes and serve.

BALEARIC OCTOPUS SOUP

6 Servings

- 1 medium-size onion
- 2–3 tomatoes
- oil
- 1 octopus (or cuttle fish)
- 2 tablespoons chopped parsley
- 1½ litres (1½ quarts) water
- salt and pepper
- bread slices

Peel and wash the onion and the tomatoes, slice them and fry in 2 tablespoons of oil in a saucepan. Clean and cut the octopus into small pieces and add to the onion and tomatoes. Fry together for 10 to 15 minutes, add parsley and water. Simmer for 2 to 3 hours. Season to taste. Fry several slices of bread per person, drop them into the soup, cook for another 15 minutes and serve.

HSAN BYOKE/BURMESE FISH SOUP

4 Servings

- 250 grs (½ lb) bass or mackerel
- 1½ tablespoons soya sauce
- pinch black pepper
- 1 litre (2 pints or 4 cups) water
- 1 teaspoon salt
- 1 onion
- 2 tablespoons rice
- 120 grs (4 oz or ⅓ cup) white cabbage
- 60 grs (2 oz or 4 tablespoons) celery
- 1 teaspoon balachaung (p 150)

Scale and wash fish, remove heads and keep. Skin and bone the fish, cut into bite-sized pieces, put in a dish, sprinkle with soya sauce and pepper and leave to steep in this dressing, turn from time to time, while you prepare the stock. Put heads, bones and skin into a pan with water. Add salt and onion, bring to the boil, reduce heat, simmer for 30 minutes and strain. Rinse out the pan, pour strained stock back into it and bring to the boil. Add rice, cook for 12 minutes, then add fish with its dressing. As soon as boiling is re-established, reduce heat and simmer gently for 12–15 minutes. Add vegetables and balachaung, cook for 5–6 minutes and serve.

HOT AND SOUR SOUP WITH FISH

6 Servings

- 6 dried Chinese mushrooms
- 1 fish, 1½–1¾ kg (3–3½ lb) (mullet, bream or sea-trout)
- 1¼ litre (2½ pints or 5 cups) water
- salt
- 6 peppercorns
- 1¼ dcl (¼ pint or ½ cup) vinegar
- 1 onion, sliced
- 2 cloves garlic
- 2–3 dried chillis
- 1 tablespoon soya sauce

Soak the mushrooms, in enough lukewarm water to cover, for 20 minutes. Drain and remove stalks.

Scale and wash the fish, but leave head and tail on. Put it in a pan or fish kettle, with water, salt, peppercorns, vinegar and onion. Bring to the boil, skim, reduce heat and simmer for 15 minutes.

Crush garlic with chillis, dilute with soya sauce, blend well and add to fish soup.

Add mushroom caps, simmer 5 minutes.

Take care not to overcook or break the fish. Place it whole on a heated serving dish. Serve soup and fish at the same time in separate bowls.

SHARKS' FIN SOUP

6–8 Servings

- 375 grs (12 oz) sharks' fins
- 1 knob 2½ cm (1 inch) fresh ginger
- 1 clove crushed garlic
- cold water
- 1 leg of chicken
- 120 grs (4 oz or ½ cup) raw breast of chicken
- 60 grs (2 oz or ¼ cup) Chinese (or smoked) ham
- 6 tablespoons bamboo shoots
- ½ litre (5 pints or 10 cups) hot chicken stock
- 2 tablespoons Shao Shing or sherry
- soya sauce
- 1 teaspoon sesame oil
- vinegar
- salt

Soak the sharks' fins in water for 24 hours. Boil them slowly for 4 hours with ginger and garlic in double the amount of water required to cover them. Drain and remove any flesh on the fins.

Put it in a basin, place the chicken leg on top and steam slowly for 2 hours. Remove the chicken leg and any water which may have dropped on the fins.

Shred chicken breast, ham and bamboo shoots into fine strips.

Put sharks' fins into saucepan, pour in enough stock to cover and boil for 5 minutes. Add chicken, ham, bamboo shoots and wine, and simmer for another 5 minutes.

Add a few drops of soya sauce, sesame oil, vinegar and salt to taste and serve.

JAPANESE LOBSTER SOUP

4 Servings

- ½ kg (1 lb) lobster
- salt
- 2 sliced leeks
- 125 grs (4 oz or ⅓ cup) shredded cabbage
- sprig chopped parsley
- shoyu
- 1 litre (2 pints) dashi (see p 21)

Cut off lobster's head and chop body into portions. Boil lobster and vegetables separately in salted water. Heat the dashi. Drain the cooked lobster chunks and vegetables, season with shoyu to taste, divide among four bowls, add piping hot dashi, and serve. Equivalent quantity of prawns may be substituted for lobster.

CRAYFISH BISQUE

6 Servings

- 150 grs (5 oz or 11½ tablespoons) rice
- 2¼ litres (2¼ quarts or 9 cups) light stock
- 2 carrots
- 1 onion
- 1 parsnip
- 150 grs (5 oz or 10 tablespoons) butter
- 1 sprig thyme
- 1 small bay leaf
- 12–18 crayfish
- salt and pepper
- 6 tablespoons brandy
- 2½ dcl (½ pint or 1 cup) dry white wine
- 120 ml (4 oz or ½ cup) cream
- pinch cayenne pepper

Wash rice carefully and cook it in 2½ cups of the stock. Meanwhile cut carrots in half, remove core, and chop finely. Chop onion and parsnip and sauté gently with carrot in 1 tablespoon butter. Add thyme and bay leaf. Increase heat, and add crayfish, salt and pepper. Sauté briskly. Pour in brandy, light it, and put out the flame by pouring on white wine. Simmer for 8 minutes. Remove from heat.

Take out half the crayfish, extract flesh from tails, and set aside in a little stock. To the other half add the hot rice, and pound until the mixture acquires a creamy consistency.

Rub through a sieve, pressing it through with a wooden spoon.

Put the purée into a saucepan and dilute with the rest of the stock. Add cream, blend, and remove from heat. Incorporate butter, and flavour with a small pinch of cayenne pepper.

Serve garnished with the remaining crayfish tails, cut into pieces. This soup should be the colour of cooked crayfish.

LOBSTER BISQUE

Follow recipe for Crayfish Bisque, substituting equivalent amount of lobster for crayfish.

FRENCH MUSSEL SOUP

4 Servings

- 2 litres (2 quarts) mussels
- 120 ml (4oz or ½ cup) dry white wine
- 2 teaspoons chopped parsley
- salt
- small bouquet garni
- butter
- 2 finely chopped onions
- 1 crushed clove garlic
- ½ litre (1 pint or 2 cups) boiling water
- 120 ml (4 oz or ½ cup) scalded milk
- 8 slices French bread
- 2 raw yolks
- 120 ml (4 oz or ½ cup) cream
- juice of 1 lemon
- pepper

Scrape and wash mussels thoroughly. Put in a pan with white wine, parsley, ½ teaspoon salt and bouquet garni. Boil for 4–5 minutes until the mussels open. Keep warm but do not allow to cook any longer, otherwise you will make the mussels rubbery.

Strain the pan juices through double muslin and keep. In a large saucepan heat 60 grs (2 oz or 4 tablespoons) butter and gently fry onions and garlic until pale golden. Add strained mussel liquor, boiling water and milk. Bring to the boil, then simmer for 15 minutes. Taste, add salt if necessary and season with pepper.

Take mussels out of their shells and add to soup.

Fry slices of bread in butter and keep hot.

Beat yolk and cream in a soup tureen, stir in lemon juice, pour hot soup over the mixture. Serve with fried bread.

JAPANESE MUSSEL SOUP

6 Servings

- 12–18 mussels
- 1½ litres (1½ quarts or 6 cups) dashi (p 21)
- 1 tablespoon soya sauce
- ½ tablespoon sake
- salt and pepper
- lemon rind

Wash the mussels with care, scrape and rinse well. Bring dashi to the boil, drop in mussels, cook until they open. Remove beards and discard shells. Strain broth through muslin and reheat. Put mussels back in the broth. Add soya sauce and sake, season to taste. Simmer for 3–4 minutes.

Pare the lemon rind very finely so no pith remains, cut into petals.

Serve soup in individual bowls decorated with lemon petals. If sake is not available, use dry sherry.

FLORIDA SEAFOOD BISQUE

6 Servings

- 240 ml (½ pint or 1 cup) light chicken stock
- 120 ml (4 oz or ½ cup) milk
- 1 tablespoon butter
- 12 fresh oysters
- a few drops Tabasco
- 120 grs (4 oz or ½ cup) flaked fresh crab meat
- 120 grs (4 oz or 1 cup) roughly chopped peeled prawns
- 2 tablespoons sherry
- salt and pepper
- pinch nutmeg
- 120 ml (4 oz or ½ cup) double cream
- ½ teaspoon paprika

In a saucepan heat stock and milk, add butter and stir to dissolve. Pour into the saucepan any liquid from the oysters, straining it carefully. Cut the oysters into bite-sized pieces.

Add oysters, Tabasco, crab meat and prawns to pan. Simmer for 10 minutes. Add sherry, season with salt and pepper, sprinkle in nutmeg. Keeping on very low heat, so that the bisque does not boil, blend in cream. Remove from heat, decant into soup bowls, sprinkle with paprika and serve piping hot.

CARIBBEAN CRAB GUMBO

4–6 Servings

- 2–3 cooked crabs or 360 grs (12 oz or 1½ cups) crab meat
- 2 tablespoons butter
- 2 tablespoons olive oil
- 1 large chopped onion
- 1 seeded, shredded green pepper
- ½ seeded, shredded red pepper
- ½ tablespoon chopped chives
- 240 grs (8 oz) okra
- 1 clove crushed garlic
- 3 large peeled chopped tomatoes
- bouquet garni
- water
- salt
- 120 ml (4 oz or ½ cup) cream

Extract crab meat, make sure there are no small pieces of shell, and flake the meat.

Heat 1 tablespoon each of butter and oil and lightly fry onion until soft. Add green and red pepper, fry together for 3–4 minutes and transfer to a large saucepan.

In remaining butter and oil lightly fry crab meat, sprinkle with chives, stir and add to onion and peppers.

Slice okra. Add okra, garlic, tomatoes and bouquet garni to saucepan. Add enough water to cover, bring to the boil and season to taste with salt. Cover and simmer for 1 hour. Remove from heat, stir in cream and serve.

The gumbo is a thick soup; thick enough to serve as a stew, with rice.

CAPE COD OYSTER SOUP

6 Servings

- 1 litre (1 quart) oysters and their liquor
- ¾ litre (1½ pints or 3 cups) milk
- salt and black pepper
- 2 tablespoons butter
- 120 ml (4 oz or ½ cup) cream
- paprika

Remove shells and strain oyster juice through double muslin into a large saucepan. Rinse oysters and add to their juices. Gently heat, simmer for 4–5 minutes on low heat. Add milk, heat almost to boiling point, season to taste with salt and freshly ground pepper. Stir in butter, adding it in small pieces. Add cream, stir and remove from heat. Check seasoning, sprinkle with paprika and serve at once.

RUSSIAN CRAYFISH AND RICE SOUP

Large freshwater crayfish is usually used for this soup in Russia. Dublin Bay or Pacific prawns are recommended.

6 Servings

- 12–18 large prawns
- salt
- 1½ litres (3 pints or 6 cups) water
- 2 sprigs dill (or parsley)
- 1 chopped onion
- 1½ tablespoons butter
- 1 tablespoon flour
- 6 tablespoons cooked rice
- 120 ml (4 oz or ½ cup) sour cream
- 1 tablespoon chopped dill or parsley

Wash prawns, put in saucepan, cover with water, add a teaspoon of salt, dill and onion. Bring to the boil and simmer gently until they change colour. Strain and keep the liquid in which the prawns were cooked. Remove flesh from tails and claws, if using Dublin Bay prawns, put into a clean saucepan, add enough of the liquid in which the prawns were cooked to cover and reserve.

Pound the rest of the prawns, i.e., legs and shells, in mortar and fry in butter stirring until the mixture acquires a dark red colour.

Sprinkle in flour, blend well and fry together for 2–3 minutes. Little by little add 2½ dcl (½ pint or 1 cup) of the liquid in which the prawns were cooked. Bring to the boil, strain through muslin and add to remaining prawn liquid. Add prawn tails and claws with their liquid and the rice. Season to taste with salt and freshly ground pepper.

Heat sour cream without boiling, add to soup. Reheat soup without allowing it to boil, sprinkle with chopped dill and serve.

CATALAN MACARONI AND MUSSEL SOUP

6 Servings

- ½ litre (1 pint or 2 cups) mussels (small ones)
- 1 tablespoon butter or oil
- 1½ litres (1½ quarts) stock
- 240 grs (8 oz. or 2 cups) cut macaroni
- 2 tablespoons tomato paste
- salt and pepper

Rinse the mussels thoroughly. Heat butter or oil in a saucepan and drop the mussels into the hot fat to open them. Remove the shells, leaving the mussels in the saucepan. Add stock, bring to the boil and put in macaroni and tomato paste. Season to taste, cook for 25 minutes and serve.

PORTUGUESE PRAWN SOUP

4 Servings

- 2–3 tablespoons olive oil
- 1 large sliced onion
- 1 sliced carrot
- 2 large peeled and chopped tomatoes
- 120 ml (4 oz or ½ cup) dry white wine
- 2 tablespoons port
- ½ kg (1 lb or 2½ cups) prawns in their shells
- 1 litre (1 quart or 4 cups) water
- 100 grs (3½ oz or ½ cup) rice
- salt and pepper
- 1 tablespoon butter

Heat oil in a saucepan and fry onion and carrot for 5 minutes. Add tomatoes, fry for a further 5 minutes. Pour in wine and port, reduce heat to simmering.

Wash prawns and add to saucepan. Cook until they turn bright pink. Add water, bring to the boil and with a perforated spoon take out prawns. Add rice to the pan, season with salt and pepper.

Shell and de-vein prawns, keep a few for garnish, pound the rest in a mortar to reduce to paste and add to pan. Simmer until the rice is done.

Rub through a sieve or purée the soup in a blender. Reheat, stir in butter adding it in small pieces and serve.

Vegetable Soups

ASPARAGUS AND SPINACH SOUP

4 Servings

- 240 grs (8 oz) tinned asparagus tips
- 250 ml (½ pint or 1 cup) chicken consommé
- 1 heaped teaspoon cornflour
- 1 packet frozen spinach (leaf or purée)
- salt and pepper
- 120 ml (4 oz or ½ cup) milk
- 30 grs (1 oz or 2 tablespoons) butter
- 120 ml (4oz or ½ cup) cream
- 1 raw yolk
- 1–2 tablespoons grated cheese
- pinch mace

Drain the asparagus and keep the juice. Cut asparagus into 2½ cm (1 inch) pieces.

Heat the consommé. Dilute cornflour with 2 tablespoons asparagus juice and stir into the consommé. Add spinach and cook for 3–4 minutes. Season to taste with salt and pepper, add remaining asparagus juice and simmer for 5 minutes. Reduce heat, add milk, stir, simmer for 1 minute. Little by little incorporate butter. Blend yolk with cream and, keeping the saucepan on lowest possible heat, stir into the soup. On no account allow the soup to boil after adding the cream and yolk mixture. Put in asparagus tips which only need heating through. Sprinkle in cheese and mace and serve.

ENGLISH WATERCRESS SOUP

4 Servings

- 1 bunch watercress
- 2 tablespoons butter
- ¾ litre (1½ pints or 3 cups) boiling water or stock
- salt and pepper
- 1 raw yolk
- 120 ml (4 oz or ½ cup) milk
- 2–3 tablespoons cream

To give this soup the maximum of flavour, keep as much of the watercress stems as possible. Wash the watercress, chop finely and in a saucepan cook lightly in butter for a couple of minutes, to soften it. Do not allow to brown. Pour on boiling water, simmer for 8–10 minutes. Season to taste.

Beat yolk with milk and, away from heat, stir the mixture into the soup. Add cream and serve.

NORWEGIAN CHERVIL SOUP

4–5 Servings

240 grs (8 oz) fresh chervil
1 litre (1 quart or 4 cups) stock
salt and pepper
2 raw yolks

for garnish:
4 or 5 lightly poached eggs
4 or 5 tablespoons cooked asparagus tips

Pick over chervil, discard stalks. Wash and drain chervil thoroughly, chop finely or put through a mincer. Heat and season stock.

Put the yolks in a soup tureen, beat, dilute with a cupful of hot but not boiling stock, then add the rest of the hot stock. Add chervil – it requires no cooking. Garnish with poached eggs and asparagus tips and serve.

FINNISH CABBAGE SOUP WITH MILK

6 Servings

1 small shredded cabbage
salt
water
1½ tablespoons butter
750 ml (1½ pints or 6 cups) milk
1 tablespoon flour
pinch sugar

Cook the cabbage, which should be white or pale green, but of the round head variety, in barely enough salted water to cover. Add butter, simmer for 10 minutes.

Mix a little milk with flour, then add the rest of the milk, blend well and pour the mixture into the pan with the cabbage.

Add sugar and season to taste. Simmer for 10 minutes and serve.

ONION SOUP

6–8 Servings

250 grs (8 oz) onions
4 tablespoons butter
1 heaped tablespoon flour
2 litres (2 quarts) stock or salted water
6–8 slices bread, dried in the oven
75 grs (2½ oz or ⅔ cup) grated Gruyere cheese

Slice the onions finely and fry in butter, stirring frequently. As soon as they acquire a slight colour, sprinkle with flour, and stir with a wooden spoon for 3 minutes. Add water or stock and simmer gently for 20 minutes. Put slices of bread in a soup tureen or in individual bowls. Sprinkle each slice with grated cheese. Strain the soup over the bread. (If preferred, the soup need not be strained.) Sprinkle with grated cheese and a little melted butter. Put in oven preheated to 220°C (450°F or Gas Regulo 7) until the cheese becomes crisp and golden.

BESSARABIAN BEETROOT SOUP WITH CHERRIES

4 Servings

- 750 grs (1½ lb or 3¼ cups) raw grated beetroot
- 750 ml (1½ pints or 3¼ cups) water
- 3–4 tablespoons lemon juice
- 1½ teaspoons salt
- 2–3 tablespoons sugar
- 240 grs (8 oz or 1¼ cups) stoned morello cherries
- 120 ml (4 oz or ½ cup) sour cream

Bring beetroot to the boil in water with lemon juice. Simmer for 20 minutes and strain, but do not press any of the beetroot through. You only want the juice which has got all the flavour by now. Add salt and sugar, heat, add cherries. Simmer for 2 minutes, remove from heat, stir in sour cream and serve.

SWISS POTATO AND CHEESE SOUP

3–4 Servings

- 2–3 medium-sized potatoes
- ½ litre (1 pint or 2 cups) stock or water
- 1 tablespoon butter
- ½ chopped onion
- 1 tablespoon flour
- 2½ dcl (½ pint or 1 cup) scalded milk
- salt and pepper
- 1 teaspoon caraway seeds
- 90 grs (3 oz or ¾ cup) grated Emmental cheese
- 2–3 tablespoons cream

Peel, slice, cook potatoes in stock until tender and mash. Heat butter, fry onion until soft, stir in flour and cook together without browning. Add to potatoes and force the whole through a sieve or pass through a blender.

Return to pan, heat, blend in milk, season to taste, add caraway seeds and cheese. Simmer until the cheese melts, stir in cream and serve with croûtons (p. 144).

ITALIAN LETTUCE SOUP

6 Servings

- 1½ tablespoons olive oil
- 1–2 cloves crushed garlic
- 2 shredded heads of lettuce—Webb's or Cos, if possible
- 1 litre (1 quart) light stock or water
- salt and pepper
- grated Parmesan cheese

Heat oil and fry garlic for 2–3 minutes. Remove garlic and in the same oil quickly toss lettuce. Transfer to a saucepan, add stock, bring to the boil, season, simmer for 2–3 minutes and serve with croûtons (p. 144) and grated cheese.

BELGIAN GREEN SOUP

4 Servings

- 1 litre (1 quart or 4 cups) consommé (p 85)
- 30 grs (1 oz or 2 tablespoons) butter
- 60 grs (2 oz or 6 tablespoons) chopped spring onions
- 2 tablespoons chopped parsley
- pinch chopped basil
- 1 bunch watercress, washed and chopped
- 1 small shredded lettuce
- salt and pepper.
- 60 ml (2 oz or 4 tablespoons) cream
- 1 tablespoon chopped chives

Skim all fat off the surface of the stock or consommé, bring it to the boil.

Heat butter in a pan large enough to take all ingredients. Add all chopped vegetables and herbs and cook gently, stirring frequently for 7–8 minutes.

Add consommé, season to taste, simmer for 25–30 minutes. Remove from heat, add cream, sprinkle in chives and serve at once.

TRANSYLVANIAN BEAN SOUP

6 Servings

- 240 grs (8 oz or 1¼ cups) dried beans
- 2½ litres (2½ quarts) bacon or ham stock
- 2 tablespoons flour
- 2½ dcl (½ pint or 1 cup) sour cream
- ½ litre (1 pint or 2 cups) milk
- 3 tablespoons vinegar
- salt and paprika
- 1–2 teaspoons dried chopped mint

Soak the beans in cold water for 3–4 hours, drain. Bring stock to the boil, add beans, simmer until tender. Dilute flour with equal amount of cold water in a bowl, add sour cream and milk, mix well and stir the mixture into the soup.

Bring to the boil, little by little add vinegar. Check seasoning, avoid oversalting. Add paprika to taste.

Put mint into a heated soup tureen, pour the soup over it and serve.

CORN CHOWDER

6 Servings

- 6 slices diced bacon
- 75 grs (2½ oz or ½ cup) finely chopped onion
- ¾ litre (1½ pints or 3 cups) water or stock
- 480 grs (1 lb) can cream-style corn
- 1 teaspoon salt
- ¼ teaspoon pepper
- ¾ litre (1½ pints or 3 cups) milk
- 2½ dcl (½ pint or 1 cup) cream
- popcorn for garnish (optional)

Fry bacon until crisp in a saucepan big enough to take all ingredients. Reserve half the bacon. To the rest add onion and sauté until soft. Add water, bring to the boil. Add corn, salt and pepper to taste and milk. Simmer for 15 minutes. Remove from heat. Stir in cream, taste for seasoning, crumble reserved bacon into soup, garnish with popcorn and serve piping hot.

SPANISH MINT SOUP

6 Servings

- 30 grs (1 oz or 2 tablespoons) olive oil
- 1 chopped onion
- 2 large peeled, chopped tomatoes
- 180 grs (6 oz) bread
- 1¼ litres (1¼ quarts) hot water
- salt
- a handful fresh mint leaves

Heat oil in saucepan and fry onion and tomatoes. Cut bread in chunks and add to onions and tomatoes. Stir once or twice to impregnate bread with the pan juices. Pour in water, season to taste with salt. Add mint, simmer for 1 hour and serve.

MIMOSA SOUP

6 Servings

- 180 grs (6 oz) French beans
- salt
- 60 grs (2 oz or 6 tablespoons) potato flour
- 1½ litres (3 pints or 6 cups) consommé (p 85)
- 2 tablespoons butter
- 3 hard-boiled yolks

Cook beans in lightly salted water until just tender, drain and keep warm. Blend potato flour with a cup of cold consommé. Heat the rest of the consommé and stir the potato flour into it. Simmer for 10 minutes, season to taste.

Put butter into a warmed soup tureen, pour in soup, mix well.

Scatter the beans on top and sprinkle with hard-boiled yolks rubbed through a large-holed sieve, to give the appearance of mimosa flowers.

ITALIAN RICE AND CABBAGE SOUP

6 Servings

- 2 tablespoons butter
- 125 grs (4 oz or ½ cup) diced pickled pork
- 250 grs (8 oz or 1 cup) peeled, diced tomatoes
- 2 tablespoons chopped parsley
- 1 clove garlic
- 500 grs (1 lb or 2¾ cups) diced cabbage
- 1½ litres (3 pints or 5 cups) beef or chicken stock
- salt and pepper
- 250 grs (8 oz or 1 cup) rice
- grated Parmesan cheese

Melt butter, add pork and fry, stirring for 3–4 minutes. Add tomatoes, parsley and garlic. Stir, cook over low heat for 5–6 minutes. Remove and discard garlic.

Add cabbage, cover and cook over low heat for 20 minutes. Season to taste, add stock, bring to the boil and simmer for 1 hour. Add rice, stir, cover and simmer for 20 minutes. Serve sprinkled with grated cheese.

BASQUE SOUP

6 Servings

- 180 grs (6 oz or 1 cup) dried haricot beans
- 2–3 tablespoons lard
- 120 grs (4 oz or ¾ cup) chopped onion
- 240 grs (8 oz or 1¼ cups) diced pumpkin
- 90 grs (3 oz or ¼ cup) shredded white cabbage
- 1–2 cloves garlic
- 2 litres (2 quarts) water
- salt and pepper

Soak the beans in enough water to cover for 2 hours. Drain well. Heat lard and brown the onion. Add pumpkin, cabbage, beans, garlic and water. Bring to the boil, season to taste, cover and simmer for 3 hours.

PORTUGUESE PEAS AND ASPARAGUS SOUP

6 Servings

- 60 grs (2 oz or 4 tablespoons) ham
- 1 tablespoon butter
- 240 grs (8 oz or 1 cup) shelled peas

- 1 litre (1 quart) stock
- 5 tablespoons tapioca
- 1 bunch of cooked asparagus (or tinned asparagus)
- salt and pepper

Chop the ham and fry lightly in a saucepan. Add peas and pour in the stock. Add tapioca and asparagus tips. (If tinned asparagus is used, it needs no cooking but just scalding with boiling water.) Season to taste. Cook for 6 or 7 minutes and serve.

BLACK BEAN SOUP

6 Servings

- ½ kg (1 lb or 2 cups) black beans
- 2½ litres (5 pints or 10 cups) water
- rind and bone of cooked smoked ham
- 90 grs (3 oz or 4 tablespoons) shredded celery
- 2 – 3 shredded leeks
- 2 thinly sliced onions
- 3–4 allspice berries
- 1 teaspoon salt
- ¼ teaspoon pepper
- 1–2 tablespoons lemon juice
- 120 ml (4 oz or ½ cup) white wine
- 1 thinly sliced lemon
- 2 chopped hard-boiled eggs

Wash beans and soak overnight in enough cold water to cover. Drain, put in a big pot with water, ham rind and bone, celery, leeks, onions and allspice. Bring to a boil, season with salt and pepper, cover and simmer gently for 2½–3 hours. Remove ham bone and rind. Rub the beans and their liquid through a sieve or purée in a blender. Return to pot, check seasoning, add lemon juice and wine and reheat to boiling point, stirring to prevent sticking.

Pour soup into a heated tureen, garnish with lemon slices, sprinkle with chopped egg and serve. This pale garnish looks most appetising and attractive floating on the surface of the rich dark soup.

RISI E BISI

This is a Venetian speciality, a soup so thick that it is almost a risotto and can be eaten with a fork.

6 Servings

- 1½ tablespoons oil
- 60grs (2 oz or 4 tablespoons) butter
- 1 small chopped onion
- 60 grs (2 oz or 4 tablespoons) chopped bacon or ham
- 2 tablespoons chopped parsley
- 1 kg (2 lb or 4 cups) shelled peas
- 1½ litres (3 pints or 6 cups) beef or chicken stock (p 18)
- salt and pepper
- ½ kg (1 lb or 2¼ cups) rice
- grated Parmesan cheese

In a saucepan heat oil with 2 tablespoons butter, add onion, bacon or ham and parsley and sweat gently, not so much to fry them as to make them yield their juices. Add peas, cook on low heat, stirring to permeate the peas with the pan juices, for 5 minutes.

Heat stock and season to taste. Add ¼ litre (½ pint or 1 cup) stock to the pan in which the peas are cooking. Bring to the boil and add rice. Pour in another ¼ litre (½ pint or 1 cup) stock, so that the rice is covered. Simmer gently for 30 minutes, without stirring, and adding more hot stock as it becomes absorbed.

As soon as the rice is done, carefully stir in the remaining butter and 2 tablespoons grated Parmesan. Serve a dish of grated Parmesan with risi e bisi.

AMERICAN CONGRESS BEAN SOUP

8 Servings

½ kg (1 lb or 2¼ cups) dried white beans
3 litres (3 quarts) water
1 meaty ham bone
3 medium-sized chopped onions
2 pounded cloves garlic
1 chopped head celery
210 grs (7 oz or 1 cup) cooked mashed potato
2 tablespoons chopped parsley
salt and pepper

Soak the beans overnight in enough cold water to cover. Drain, put in a big saucepan with water and the ham bone. There should be enough meat on the bone to garnish the soup after cooking. Bring to the boil and cook for 2 hours. Add the rest of the ingredients, season to taste and simmer for 1½ hours, or until the beans are tender. Take out ham bone, cut the meat off it, slice and add to soup. Serve piping hot.

KANSAS WALNUT SOUP

This recipe dates back to the American pioneering days. According to the report of the Kansas American Association, this soup was developed when black walnuts were all the women could get to cook, other crops having been killed by droughts. There appeared to be no shortage of dairy produce!

6 Servings

180 grs (6 oz or 1½ cups) shelled chopped walnuts
90 ml (3 oz or 6 tablespoons) sour cream
180 grs (6 oz or 1½ cups) flour
pinch dried sage
60 grs (2 oz or 4 tablespoons) butter
1¼ litres (1¼ quarts) hot stock (p 17–18)
salt and pepper
180 ml (6 oz or ¾ cup) double cream

Pound the walnuts, add sour cream, 2½ tablespoons flour and sage and mix well.

In a saucepan heat butter, stir in remaining flour, cook a pale golden roux, gradually blend in stock. Bring to the boil, season to taste with salt and pepper. Reduce heat, little by little add walnut mixture, stirring it in. Simmer for 10 minutes, stirring constantly. Remove from heat, add cream, stir and serve.

SPANISH HAZELNUT SOUP

This recipe comes from the Avenida Palace Hotel, Barcelona.

6 Servings

- 180 grs (6 oz or 2 cups) shelled, peeled and toasted hazelnuts
- 60 grs (2 oz or 4 tablespoons) butter
- 30 grs (1 oz or 4 tablespoons) flour
- 1 litre (2 pints or 4 cups) hot consommé (p 85)
- 2 raw yolks
- 120 ml (4 oz or ½ cup) double cream
- salt and pepper

Grind the hazelnuts finely. In a saucepan heat butter, add hazelnuts and flour, cook stirring for a few seconds to mix.

Add consommé, stir well. Bring to the boil, simmer gently for 15 minutes, stirring all the time.

Beat yolks with cream, dilute with a ladle of warm soup, stir into the soup keeping it on lowest possible heat. Reheat without allowing it to come to the boil. Season to taste and serve.

CORN AND WATERCRESS SOUP

4 Servings

- 1 litre (2 pints or 4 cups) beef stock
- 1 teaspoon chopped parsley
- ¼ teaspoon marjoram
- ½ kg (1 lb or 2 cups) corn scraped from the cob (or frozen corn)
- 1 bunch chopped watercress
- salt and pepper
- 2–3 tablespoons butter
- 2 chopped hard-boiled eggs

Bring the stock to the boil with parsley and marjoram. Add corn and simmer for 30 minutes. Rub through a sieve or purée the soup in a blender. Add watercress, season to taste, stir and heat. Gradually incorporate butter, blending it in in small pieces.

Serve sprinkled with chopped hard-boiled eggs.

ONION SOUP WITH CHAMPAGNE AND CAMEMBERT

6 Servings

- 60 grs (2 oz or 4 tablespoons) butter
- 4 sliced onions
- $\frac{3}{4}$ litre ($1\frac{1}{2}$ pints or 3 cups) beef stock (p 17)
- salt and pepper
- pinch mace
- $\frac{1}{2}$ litre (1 pint or 2 cups) champagne
- 5 tablespoons ripe Camembert cheese
- 3 eggs
- 60 ml (2 oz or 4 tablespoons) port
- 3 tablespoons finely chopped walnuts

Heat butter in a saucepan and brown onions. Pour in stock, season, add mace and simmer for 15 minutes.

Add champagne, heat the soup and stir in Camembert. Simmer for 2 minutes.

Beat eggs with port. Remove soup from heat, stir in eggs. Ladle into individual plates, sprinkle with walnuts and serve.

Clear Soups with Garnishes

CONSOMMÉ

In classical French cuisine a consommé is a lightly salted stock, enriched, concentrated and clarified.

To make 6 litres (6 quarts) of chicken consommé:

6 litres (6 quarts) chicken stock
¾ kg (1½ lb) chicken meat and bones
1 set chicken giblets
1 diced carrot
1–2 sliced leeks
1 raw white of egg

Chop the chicken meat, bones and giblets and put in a muslin bag. This helps to avoid little bones getting past, or stuck in, the strainer.

Put the meat, bones and giblets in a large pot, add carrots, leeks and white of egg. Stir to mix well.

Add stock, which can be cold or hot, stirring with a wooden spoon. Slowly bring to the boil, while you continue to stir.

As soon as boiling is established, reduce heat and simmer gently for 1–1½ hours. This will give the additional meat and vegetables time to enrich the stock.

Strain through a cloth dipped in cold water and thoroughly wrung out.

Consommés are thickened with arrowroot, cornflour or tapioca, but this liaison should be very light, otherwise the texture of the consommé will be coarsened. The best liaison is poached tapioca. For 1 litre (1 quart) of consommé, allow 3 tablespoons of poached tapioca, strained through a muslin bag to ensure clarity.

CONSOMMÉ WITH SHREDDED CHICKEN AND LETTUCE

4–5 Servings
2 litres (2 quarts) consommé thickened with tapioca

4 tablespoons cooked chicken breast, cut in fine julienne strips
2 dozen small chicken quenelles (p 143)
1 lettuce heart, shredded in a chiffonade

Bring the consommé to the boil with the poached and strained tapioca.

Into a heated soup tureen put chicken, quenelles and lettuce. Pour boiling consommé on top of this garnish and serve at once.

CONSOMMÉ PRINTANIER

Prepare enriched, clarified consommé. Garnish with 2 tablespoons each young turnips and carrots, scooped out with a small ball scoop or cut in small dice, and the same quantity of shelled fresh garden peas and sliced green beans, all cooked in a little stock or lightly salted water and drained.

Sprinkle with a pinch of chopped chervil or parsley before serving.

CONSOMMÉ BASQUE STYLE

6 Servings

4 tablespoons rice
2 tablespoons diced peeled tomatoes cut in julienne strips
2 tablespoons sweet peppers peeled
2 litres (2 quarts) consommé
1 tablespoon chopped chervil

Cook the rice, tomatoes and peppers separately in a little stock. Strain, put in heated soup tureen. Pour boiling consommé on the garnish, sprinkle with chervil and serve.

CONSOMMÉ BOUQUETIERE

6 Servings

2 litres (2 quarts) consommé, thickened with poached, strained tapioca
2 tablespoons cooked turnips and carrots, scooped out with a small ball scoop, or cut in small dice
2 tablespoons French beans, cooked and cut into lozenges
2 tablespoons cooked asparagus tips

Put the cooked strained vegetables into a soup tureen and pour boiling consommé over the garnish. Serve at once.

CONSOMMÉ ROYALE

Royale is the French name for moulded custard used as garnish for clear soups.

6 Servings

- 2 litres (2 quarts) chicken consommé thickened with poached tapicoa
- 4 eggs
- $\frac{1}{4}$ litre ($\frac{1}{2}$ pint or 1 cup) milk
- $\frac{1}{4}$ litre ($\frac{1}{2}$ pint or 1 cup) skimmed chicken stock
- pinch salt
- pinch grated nutmeg

Beat the eggs and strain through a fine strainer. Add milk and stock, both of which should be hot but not boiling. Season with salt and nutmeg, stir well and pour into a shallow mould or pie dish.

Stand the mould in a bain-marie and put in the oven, pre-heated to 175°C 350°F (Gas Regulo 3). Cook until the savoury custard sets and is firm to the touch.

Leave until quite cold, then turn out on to a cloth and either dice neatly or cut into squares, rounds, stars, leaves, or any other shapes.

Bring consommé to the boil. Gently drop the royale garnish into it and serve at once.

RICE CONSOMMÉ

Wash rice and cook in stock, allowing half a tablespoon of raw rice per portion. Take care not to overcook – the appearance of the soup will be spoilt if the grains are not separate. Drain and add to well seasoned consommé. Just before serving sprinkle with chopped chervil or parsley.

CONSOMMÉ AU DIABLOTINS

Chicken consommé thickened with tapioca and served with diablotins.

To make diablotins: cut French bread into thin round slices, cover with a mixture of thick Béchamel sauce (p. 22) flavoured with grated cheese and a dash of cayenne pepper. Sprinkle with grated Parmesan cheese and brown the top in the oven or under the grill.

CONSOMMÉ SCOTTISH STYLE

Unthickened chicken consommé with pearl barley cooked in the consommé, garnished with carrot, celery and leeks, cut in thin strips and lightly cooked in butter. Serve sprinkled with chopped chervil.

CONSOMMÉ BIZET

Chicken consommé thickened with tapioca (p. 85), garnished with small chicken quenelles (p. 143) flavoured with chopped tarragon leaves. Sprinkle with chopped chervil before serving.

CONSOMMÉ COLBERT

Chicken consommé garnished with diced spring vegetables and small poached eggs, allowing one egg per portion.

CONSOMMÉ LORETTE

Chicken consommé garnished with asparagus tips, cooked in stock, and small diced bread croûtons, baked in the oven.

CONSOMMÉ CHASSEUR

Game consommé, thickened with tapioca, garnished with 2 tablespoons of mushrooms, cut in thin strips and simmered with 2–3 tablespoons Madeira, and chervil leaves.

ANGEL HAIR CONSOMMÉ

Chicken consommé garnished with very fine poached vermicelli.

CONSOMMÉ WITH FARFEL

Beef or chicken consommé garnished with farfel (p. 146).

CONSOMMÉ CHILEAN STYLE

Chicken consommé garnished with rice cooked in stock and diced green peppers also cooked in stock, sprinkled with chervil leaves.

CONSOMMÉ WITH SHREDDED OMELETTE

Prepare consommé in the usual way. Beat seasoned eggs and fry a thin flat pancake omelette. Roll it up and shred. Sprinkle shredded omelette on each plate or bowl of consommé.

CONSOMMÉ A LA CRECY

Chicken consommé, thickened with tapioca, garnished with diced young carrots, simmered in butter and a little stock.

CONSOMMÉ WITH LIVER BALLS

Beef or chicken consommé garnished with liver balls (p. 143).

All of the above are classical consommé recipes, but they can be varied by adding a different garnish of your choice. Garnishes can range from the wildly extravagant, such as foie gras quenelles (moulded and poached in exactly the same way as chicken quenelles) to a simple garnish of some pasta product or whatever vegetables are available.

Recipes for the following garnishes for beef or chicken consommés are also given :–

Meat balls (p. 146).
Almond dumplings (p. 147).
Matzo meat dumplings (p. 146).
Soup nuts (p. 145).

CLEAR BORSCH WITH CHERRY VARENIKI

6–8 Servings

Prepare borsch as described in recipe for Jewish Sour Cream Borsch (p. 109) but do not pass through a blender. Merely strain the soup, add reserved beetroot to intensify colour, as described. Do not stir in sour cream, add it at table.

Make vareniki with cherries (p. 145).

Bring borsch to the boil. Put in vareniki, a few at a time, allowing the soup to come to the boil before adding any more. Simmer for 10 minutes and serve. If you have too many vareniki, keep half to serve as a dessert for another day (see p. 145).

RAVIOLI IN BRODO

Ravioli is one of the many varieties of Italian pasta envelopes filled with various ingredients. Most people know them as pasta asciuta, but they are equally popular and delicious served in clear broth.

Ravioli can be made of ordinary noodle paste, but proper ravioli paste should contain a little butter.

6–8 Servings

- Ravioli (p 144)
- 1½–2 litres (1½–2 quarts or 6–8 cups) boiling consommé
- grated Parmesan cheese

Make ravioli as described, cook in boiling consommé and serve with a sprinkling of grated cheese.

CHINESE MEAT BALL SOUP

4 Servings

- 240 grs (8 oz or 1 cup) minced lean pork
- 1 dessertspoon of Shao Shing Chinese wine or dry sherry
- 1 tablespoon soya sauce
- 1 finely chopped leek (white part only)
- 2½ cm (1 inch) piece fresh minced ginger
- 1 tablespoon cornflour
- 1 beaten egg
- 1 litre (2 pints or 4 cups) stock
- 1 teaspoon salt
- 1 tablespoon chopped spring onion

Combine pork, wine, soya sauce, leek, ginger and cornflour. Add egg, mix well and taking a little of the mixture at a time shape into small balls.

Bring stock to the boil, season with salt to taste, drop the meat balls into it, simmer for 10–12 minutes, sprinkle with spring onions and serve.

TA PIN LO BROTH

This is variously known as Mongol Hot Pot, Japanese Hakotsu, Korean Sinsullo. The original Chinese variation is called Ta Pin Lo, 'Fire Kettle' and, with the minimum of work the hostess, provides a delightful informal meal ending with the broth.

Normally the pin lo has a charcoal burner, though gas and electric appliances exist on the market. I think charcoal types are best.

Once the charcoal brazier is well lit, sprinkle it with coarse salt, put it in the centre part of the pin lo. Stand the pin lo on a mat in the middle of the dining table and fill the outer ring with a clear stock, seasoned to taste.

Arrange your selection of thinly sliced raw food and the assortment of sauces and condiments, all of which are available from Chinese food shops, around the pin lo. Each guest has a bowl and spoon, a pair of chopsticks and a long handled wire ladle, in which they cook their food in the broth. If you have no wire ladles, use long bamboo chopsticks for cooking.

When all the ingredients have been cooked, the guests drink the broth, which is invariably delicious.

6–8 Servings

240 gr (8 oz or 1 cup) sliced chicken fillet
2 sole fillets
180 grs (6 oz or ¾ cup) calf or chicken liver
240 grs (8 oz or 1 cup) lean pork
180 grs (6 oz or ¾ cup) fillet steak
3–4 scallops
240 grs (8 oz or 1 cup) raw prawns
180 grs (6 oz or ½ cup) white cabbage
180 grs (6 oz or ½ cup) spinach or lettuce
120 grs (4 oz or 1½ cups) fresh mushrooms
120 grs (4 oz or 1½ cups) bamboo shoots
120 grs (4 oz) transparent noodles
180 grs (6 oz) bean curd
2 dozen wun tun (see p 93)
small bunch spring onions
1 tablespoon cornflour
2 tablespoons Shao Shing Wine or dry sherry
2 tablespoons water

Condiments for dipping:
light soya sauce
Chinese vinegar
sesame paste
shrimp sauce
chilli sauce
plum sauce

2 litres (4 pints or 8 cups) clear stock
salt and pepper
6–8 lettuce 'cups' (optional)
6–8 raw eggs (optional)

Cut the chicken, sole, liver, pork, steak and scallops into wafer thin slices. Shell prawns, cut in half length-wise, remove black digestive track. Cut cabbage into bite-sized pieces, put in a bowl, cover with boiling water, leave to stand for 5–6 minutes and drain well. Pick over spinach leaves. Slice mushrooms and bamboo shoots. Drop the noodles into boiling water, allow to stand for half a minute and drain. Cut bean curd into square slices. Cut spring onions into 5 cm (2 inch) lengths, then slice in half length-wise. Blend cornflour with wine and water. Arrange chicken, liver, pork and steak in a symmetrical pattern on two dishes. Lay out sole, prawns and scallops similarly on two other dishes. Sprinkle all these with cornflour and sherry mixture. Divide all the other sliced ingredients, the wun-tun and the noodles also in duplicate dishes – this will enable your guests to help themselves to everything without having to stretch across the hot pot. Check the stock for seasoning before you pour it into the pin lo and set it on the table. Arrange all your ingredients and condiments around the pin lo. Each diner helps himself to the morsel he wants, cooks it in the simmering stock, dips it in the condiments of his choice to season and cool it, and eats it. None of the ingredients need more than 45–60 seconds to cook through, except the wun-tun (see p. 93).

Noodles should be cooked last of all. The eggs should be lightly poached in the broth and it is best done by floating the lettuce 'cups' on the surface of the broth, then gently breaking an egg into each one. When all the food has been eaten, cook the noodles and serve with the soup.

This is a very splendid Ta Pin Lo. You can vary the ingredients according to whatever is available or in season. You could omit wun-tun, or the poached eggs.

FRENCH CHESTNUT SOUP

4 Servings

- 1 kg (2 lb) large chestnuts
- 1 litre (2 pints or 4 cups) consommé (p 85)
- 1 teaspoon sugar
- salt
- 30 grs (1 oz or 2 tablespoons) butter

Peel and skin chestnuts as described in recipe for Italian Chestnut Soup. Put them in small saucepan, cover with half the consommé, add sugar, season with salt, bring to the boil. Add butter, cover, reduce heat and simmer gently without stirring for 1 hour.

Heat the rest of the consommé. Add chestnuts, which should by now have absorbed all the liquid. Check seasoning and serve.

RUSSIAN SOUP WITH KLYOTSKI

6 Servings

- 1½ litres (3 pints or 6 cups) consommé (p 85)
- 120 grs (4 oz or ½ cup) semolina
- salt and pepper
- 1 tablespoon butter
- 2 eggs
- 1 tablespoon chopped dill or parsley

Measure out 120 ml (4 oz or ½ cup) consommé and bring to the boil. Pour semolina into it, stir, season with salt and pepper and add butter. Reduce heat and simmer until semolina thickens – about 6–7 minutes. Remove from heat. Separate whites from yolks. Add yolks to the semolina mixture and mix well. Whisk whites until stiff and fold into the mixture.

10 minutes before you wish to serve the soup, bring the rest of the consommé to the boil. Using a teaspoon, dip it in a cup of cold water, scoop up half a teaspoonful of the mixture and shake it off into the boiling soup. Continue in this way until all klyotski are done. Simmer gently and as soon as they float up to the surface, they are ready. Sprinkle with dill and serve.

WUN TUN/CHINESE RAVIOLI SOUP

6 Servings

For wun tun paste

480 grs (1 lb or 4 cups) flour
2 eggs
water

For filling

30 grs (1 oz) dried mushrooms
700 grs ($1\frac{1}{2}$ lb) pork
salt
180 grs (6 oz or $1\frac{1}{4}$ cups) shelled prawns
125 grs (4 oz or $\frac{3}{4}$ cup) spring onions
$\frac{1}{2}$ teaspoon Ve-Tsin
1 dessertspoon cornflour
2 dessertspoon soya sauce
1 dessertspoon brandy
1 teaspoon oil
2 eggs
2 litres (2 quarts) stock

Mix flour with eggs, gradually adding enough water to make a pliable dough.

Soak mushrooms in cold water for 3–4 hours. Drain.

Mince the pork and then season with salt to taste. Scald and shred the mushrooms, discarding stalks. Chop prawns and spring onions. Cut the dough into 5 cm (2 inch) squares. Combine pork, mushrooms, prawns, Ve-Tsin, and three-quarters of the spring onions, cornflour, soya sauce, brandy, oil and 1 egg. Blend well. Place a teaspoon of this mixture on the dough. Fold over, seal with beaten egg and round off the edge of the wun tun. Bring stock to the boil, put in wun tun a few at a time, boil fast for 7 minutes, keeping the pan uncovered, and serve sprinkled with remaining spring onions.

CHINESE WINTER MELON OR MARROW SOUP

4–6 Servings

30 grs (1 oz) dried mushrooms
120 grs (4 oz or $\frac{1}{2}$ cup) bamboo shoots
120 grs (4 oz or $\frac{1}{2}$ cup) lean ham or bacon
2–$2\frac{1}{2}$ kg (4–5 lb) winter melon (or marrow)
240 grs (8 oz or 1 cup) shredded raw chicken
240 grs (8 oz or 1 cup) shredded raw pork
$\frac{1}{4}$ teaspoon Ve-Tsin
1 knob green ginger

Blanch mushrooms and cut into thin strips. Dice the bamboo shoots and cut ham in shreds. Cut top off melon and remove some pulp and seeds to enlarge the cavity.

Boil chicken, pork, Ve-Tsin, ginger, mushrooms and bamboo shoots, together with any bones, in enough water to cover, then simmer gently for 40 minutes.

Remove all bones from soup, add ham, and pour the whole inside the melon, replacing the top.

Place the melon in a large pudding basin to keep it upright and steam for 1½ hours or until melon is completely cooked. Serve whole.

The melon is placed on the table, and as melon and soup are scooped out the melon peel is cut down to the required level. If more soup is needed it can be heated and added to the melon.

JAPANESE TREFOIL AND TRIANGULAR EGG SOUP

4 Servings

- 4 sheets foolscap paper
- 4 eggs
- 12 trefoils (Japanese green vegetable with 3 leaves)
- 4 Japanese pepper sprouts
- 1 litre (2 pints or 4 cups) seasoned clear stock

Fold the sheets of paper in half, then in half once more; holding three layers together, separate one and break an egg into each pointed pocket. (I have tried using plastic bags instead of paper, but find them too pliable and apt to tilt.) Stand the pockets, points downward, in a pan of boiling water. Cook for 7 minutes then take out of water but do not remove from paper. Chill, remove paper, and you will have four triangular hard-boiled eggs.

Tie the trefoils in bundles of three, trim to uniform length, dip into boiling salted water, then into cold water, and drain.

Trim eggs to remove any untidy edges, put one in each bowl, pour in hot stock, decorate with trefoil and pepper sprouts, cover the bowl with its lid, and serve. This soup looks most attractive in black-lined lacquer bowls.

If Japanese pepper sprouts are not available, use a small piece of lemon peel cut into suitable decorative shape. Watercress can be stripped down to resemble trefoil.

JAPANESE CUCUMBER AND EGG SOUP

4 Servings

- 1 litre (2 pints or 4 cups) dashi
- 1½ teaspoons shoyu
- 1½ teaspoons salt
- 1 cucumber peeled and sliced
- 4 eggs

Heat the dashi, season with shoyu and salt, add cucumber, cook for 3 minutes. Break eggs, one at a time, into a cup and carefully slip into the boiling dashi so that they float over the cucumber. Simmer gently long enough just to set the eggs, without stirring, and serve in individual bowls. 125 grs (4 oz or ½ cup) shelled peas or fresh beans may be substituted for cucumber.

SPANISH SPINACH SOUP

6 Servings

1 kg (2 lb) spinach
1 egg, beaten
salt and pepper
1 tablespoon butter
1 tablespoon flour
1½ litres (1½ quarts) stock
strained and seasoned

Wash the spinach and cook in 2–3 tablespoons water for 20 minutes. Drain and chop the spinach, mix in a beaten egg and season to taste. Put into a shallow oven dish, greased with butter and sprinkled with flour, and bake in a low oven until it sets. Let it cool, remove from the mould, cut into squares and serve in very hot stock.

Creamed Soups

POTAGE CRECY (FRENCH CARROT SOUP)

4 Servings

- 30 grs (1 oz or 2 tablespoons) butter
- 1 small chopped onion
- 375 grs (12 oz or 1 cup) shredded carrots
- 240 grs (8 oz or 1¼ cups) peeled sliced potato
- salt and pepper
- pinch sugar
- 750 ml (1½ pints or 3 cups) chicken stock (p 18)
- 1 tablespoon chopped parsley
- ½ tablespoon chopped chervil

In a saucepan melt butter and lightly fry onion, without browning. Add carrots and potatoes, season with salt and pepper, cook on moderate heat, uncovered, for 5 minutes, stirring. Add sugar, cover, reduce heat to the minimum and simmer gently for 10–12 minutes. Add stock, simmer for 15 minutes. Rub through a sieve or purée in a blender. Reheat the soup, add parsley and chervil and serve.

CREAM OF MUSHROOM SOUP

4 Servings

- 375 grs (12 oz) mushrooms
- 2 chopped onions
- 90 grs (3 oz or 6 tablespoons) butter
- 2 tablespoons flour
- ½ litre (1 pint or 2 cups) milk
- salt and pepper
- 120 ml (4 oz or ½ cup) cream

Reserve 120 grs (4 oz) mushroom caps, chop the rest. Fry chopped mushrooms and onion in half the butter and rub through a sieve or purée in a blender. Slice reserved mushroom caps and fry in remaining butter until soft. Sprinkle in flour, cook, stirring for 2 minutes, without allowing the mixture to brown. Dilute with milk, stirring it in a little at a time. Simmer for 5 minutes stirring, add mushroom and onion purée and season to taste. Remove from heat, blend in cream and serve at once.

CREAM OF TOMATO SOUP

4 Servings

- 1 kg (2 lbs) tomatoes
- 1 finely chopped onion
- 60 grs (2 oz or 4 tablespoons) butter
- pinch mixed herbs
- 4 tablespoons boiling water
- 2 tablespoons flour
- ½ litre (1 pint or 2 cups) milk
- 2 teaspoons sugar
- salt and pepper
- 2–3 tablespoons cream

Cut up the tomatoes roughly. Heat half the butter and fry onion until soft. Add tomatoes and herbs, stir, pour in boiling water, cover and cook on very low heat for 15 minutes. Rub through a sieve.

Heat remaining butter, stir in flour and cook together for 2–3 minutes. Gradually add milk, bring to the boil, add tomato purée, sugar and salt and pepper to taste. Simmer for 5 minutes. Remove from heat, blend in cream and serve at once with croûtons (p. 144).

CREAM OF WATERCRESS SOUP

6 Servings

- ½ kg (1 lb) watercress
- 2 tablespoons butter
- 240 grs (8 oz or 1¼ cups) diced potatoes
- 1 litre (1 quart or 4 cups) chicken stock
- 2½ dcl (½ pint or 1 cup) boiled milk
- salt
- 2–3 tablespoons cream

Wash the cress carefully, chop up coarsely, and simmer gently in butter for a few minutes. As soon as it softens, add potatoes, moisten with stock and simmer for 20 minutes. Rub through a sieve into a saucepan, or pass through a blender, bring to a boil, dilute to desired consistency with milk, and incorporate cream at the last moment.

GREEN SHCHI

'Beautiful soup, so rich and green, waiting in a hot tureen!'

This excellent spinach soup, served with its traditional accompaniments of cream cheese tartlets and hard-boiled or stuffed eggs, can make a meal in itself, as do a great many Russian soups. The egg garnish is a must. Half a hard-boiled egg looks very good in the green soup with a small island of sour cream floating beside it. But it may be kinder to one's guests to chop the eggs roughly, for even a halved egg can be treacherous.

In Russia, in the provinces, in their big-eating generous way, whole eggs were served. The great Chaliapin tells of an embarrassing moment when, as a struggling young singer, he was invited to dinner at a house of a wealthy family on whom he was anxious to make a good impression. The table was beautifully laid and green shchi was the soup course. Chaliapin was very hungry. Green shchi was one of his favourite soups. He attacked his egg, which rebelled against the pressure of the spoon, leapt out of his plate and landed in a shower of green splashes on the immaculate white damask tablecloth.

6 Servings

- 1½ litres (1½ quarts or 6 cups) beef or chicken consomme (p 85)
- 750 grs (1½ lb) spinach or 1 large packet frozen spinach
- 2 tablespoons butter
- 1 medium-sized chopped onion
- 1 medium-sized shredded carrot
- 1 medium-sized shredded turnip
- ½ medium-sized shredded parsnip
- 1 stalk shredded celery
- 1 teaspoon salt
- ½ teaspoon pepper
- 1 teaspoon sugar
- 1–2 tablespoons lemon juice
- 3 halved hard-boiled eggs or stuffed eggs (p 141)
- 120 ml (4 oz or ½ cup) sour cream
- 1–2 tablespoons chopped dill or parsley
- cream cheese tartlets (p 140)

Strain consommé and remove all fat.

Pick over and wash spinach thoroughly. Put in a saucepan with 1–2 tablespoons water and simmer for 5 minutes. Remove from heat. If you are using frozen spinach, choose leaf spinach in preference to chopped, even though the soup has to be puréed ultimately. It gives a better texture.

Heat butter and lightly fry onion, carrot, turnip, parsnip and celery to soften and seal in their juices. Do not allow to brown. Put spinach and whatever liquid has accumulated with it into a big saucepan, add all vegetables, consommé, salt, pepper and sugar. Bring to the boil, simmer for 20 minutes.

Rub through a sieve or purée in a blender, reheat. Taste for seasoning, sharpen with lemon juice and serve piping hot. If you are serving plain hard-boiled eggs, put half an egg in each plate, add a spoonful of sour cream and sprinkle with dill.

If you are serving stuffed eggs, serve them on a side plate along with the cream cheese tartlets.

NETTLE SOUP

Follow recipe for Green Shchi (p. 98), but blanch picked-over nettles in boiling water for 2 minutes. Drain, chop, fry in 1 tablespoon butter, then proceed as described.

SOUBISE SOUP WITH GARLIC BREAD

6 Servings

- ¾ kg (1½ lb) onions
- salt
- butter
- white pepper
- ½ teaspoon grated nutmeg
- pinch sugar
- 180 ml (6 oz or ¾ cup) dry white wine
- 180 ml (6 oz or ¾ cup) veal or chicken stock
- 3 tablespoons grated Parmesan cheese
- ½ litre (1 pint or 2 cups) thick Béchamel sauce (p 22)
- 120 ml (4 oz or ½ cup) cream
- 1 long French loaf
- garlic butter (p 24)

Slice onions and blanch in well-salted water for 2 minutes. Drain, put into a pan with 120 grs (4 oz or ½ cup) melted butter, a pinch of salt, sugar and nutmeg. Simmer gently until onions are tender, without allowing them to colour. Stir in Béchamel sauce, simmer for 10 minutes and rub through a fine sieve or purée in a blender. Return to saucepan, add wine and stock, bring to the boil, add cheese, stir. Reduce heat so that the soup does not come to the boil again. Blend in cream and little by little incorporate 1–2 tablespoons butter. Cut the loaf on a slant into portions down to the bottom crust, but without cutting right through. With a knife insert some garlic butter in each cut and press together to make the loaf look uncut. Do not be mean with the garlic butter. Wrap in kitchen foil and put in a very moderate oven 175°C (350°F or Gas Regulo 3) for a few minutes, to heat through. Serve with the soup.

SOUP ESTELA D'ACCURZIO

This is an Argentine speciality and one of the most palatable ways of presenting pumpkin.

4 Servings

- 750 grs (1½ lb or 3½ cups) diced pumpkin
- ½ litre (1 pint or 2 cups) light veal or chicken stock
- 1 finely chopped onion
- 2 tablespoons butter
- ¼ litre (½ pint or 1 cup) scalded milk
- salt and pepper
- 120 ml (4 oz or ½ cup) double cream
- 2 tablespoons seeded diced sweet red pepper

Cook pumpkin in stock until tender.

Fry onion in butter until soft, add to pumpkin and together force through a sieve or purée in a blender. Return to heat, stir in milk, season to taste with salt and freshly grated black pepper. Blend in cream, remove from heat and serve at once.

SORREL SOUP

These summer soups are popular in the Baltic countries, in Russia, Poland, the Ukraine and Rumania. They can be made with meat or chicken stock, or the liquid can be a mixture of milk and water.

6 Servings

- 250 grs (8 oz) fresh sorrel leaves
- 15 grs (½ oz 4 tablespoons) parsley
- 2 tablespoons butter
- 1 litre (1 quart) water
- 3–4 potatoes
- salt and pepper
- pinch sugar
- ½ litre (1 pint or 2 cups) milk
- 1–2 yolks
- 1–2 tablespoons lemon juice
- 1 carton sour cream

Wash and chop sorrel and parsley. Heat butter in a pan large enough to take all ingredients. Add sorrel and parsley and cook on low heat, stirring for 10 minutes.

Peel and dice potatoes, add to sorrel soup, season to taste with salt and pepper, add sugar, bring to boil, cover, reduce heat and simmer on low heat for 25 minutes.

Strain and keep the soup stock.

Rub the sorrel and potatoes through a sieve or pass through a blender, with half the milk, to make a smooth purée.

Reheat stock, add sorrel purée, simmer for a few minutes to heat through.

Dilute yolks with remaining milk and blend into the soup. Reheat, without allowing the soup to boil, check seasoning. Remove from heat, sharpen with lemon juice to taste and serve with a tablespoon of sour cream for each helping and cream cheese tartlets (p. 140).

CHILEAN AVOCADO SOUP

4 Servings

- 240 grs (8 oz or 1¼ cups) avocado flesh
- 2 tablespoons lemon juice
- 120 ml (4 oz or ½ cup) dry white wine
- 1 litre (2 pints or 4 cups) chicken consommé (p 85)
- 4 tablespoons sour cream
- salt and pepper

for garnish

- 2–3 tablespoons diced avocado
- 4–6 thin slices of lemon

Mash the avocado flesh with lemon juice. Heat wine and consommé separately. Combine mashed avocado, wine and consommé. Rub through a sieve or purée in a blender. Season to taste with salt and pepper. Reheat, blend in sour cream and serve with a spoonful of avocado and lemon slice in each plate.

RUMANIAN LEEK AND SORREL SOUP

4 Servings

- 4 shredded leeks, white part only
- 2 chopped onions
- 60 gr (2 oz or 4 tablespoons) butter
- 1 litre (1 quart) meat stock
- 240 grs (8 oz) chopped sorrel
- 2 medium-sized, sliced potatoes
- 1 shredded lettuce
- salt and paprika
- 120 ml (4 oz or ½ cup) cream
- 1 tablespoon chopped chives
- 1 tablespoon chopped dill or parsley

Cook leeks and onion gently in butter until soft. Do not allow to brown. Add stock, bring to the boil. Add sorrel and potatoes, cook for 10 minutes. Add lettuce, season with salt and paprika to taste and simmer for 5–6 minutes. Strain and rub the vegetables into the pan through a sieve or purée in a blender. Return to heat, bring to the boil, check seasoning. Stir in cream and remove from heat. Sprinkle with chives and dill and serve.

BAVARIAN CREAMED LIVER SOUP

6 Servings

- 60 grs (1 oz or 2 tablespoons) butter
- 1 finely chopped onion
- ½ kg (1 lb or 2 cups) diced calf liver
- 1½ tablespoons flour
- 1 litre (2 pints or 4 cups) stock
- salt and pepper
- pinch mace
- 120 grs (4 oz or ½ cup) sour cream

Heat butter in a saucepan and fry onion until soft. Add liver and brown. Sprinkle in flour, blend well, cook on low heat for 3–4 minutes. Little by little add stock. Season to taste with salt and pepper, add mace and simmer for 30 minutes.

Drain the liver and mince or pass through a blender. Return to soup, reheat, stir and serve with a topping of sour cream.

ITALIAN CHESTNUT SOUP

4 Servings

- ½ kg (1 lb) chestnuts
- 1 litre (1 quart or 4 cups) stock
- 2 tablespoons chopped lean smoked ham
- 1 bay leaf
- 1–2 cloves
- salt and pepper

Score the chestnuts with a sharp knife, put in a moderate oven 190° (375°F or Gas Regulo 4) for 15 minutes. Pull off the outer and inner skins.

Put the chestnuts in a saucepan with stock, ham, bay leaf and cloves. Simmer for 45 – 50 minutes, or until chestnuts are tender. Season to taste with salt and freshly grated black pepper. Rub through a sieve or purée in a blender. Serve with croûtons (p. 144).

SWEDISH SPLIT PEA SOUP

6 Servings

- 480 grs (1 lb or 2 cups) split peas
- 3 litres (3 quarts) bacon or ham stock
- 1 large chopped onion
- 2 chopped carrots
- 2 chopped stalks celery
- pinch ginger
- 1 tablespoon butter

Soak the peas in enough cold water to cover overnight. Drain, bring to the boil in stock, skim, add onion, carrots and celery and simmer for 2½ hours.

Check seasoning, bacon or ham stock is usually salty enough.

Sprinkle in ginger, simmer until peas are soft. Rub through a sieve or purée the soup in a blender, reheat and just before serving stir in butter, adding it in small pieces.

JERUSALEM ARTICHOKE SOUP

4 Servings

- ½ kg (1 lb) Jerusalem artichokes
- 1 chopped onion
- 2–3 stalks shredded celery
- 90 grs (3 oz or 6 tablespoons) butter or margarine
- 2½ dcl (½ pint or 1 cup) boiling water
- 3 tablespoons flour
- ½ litre (1 pint or 2 cups) milk
- salt and white pepper
- 4 tablespoons cream

Peel and slice artichokes thinly. In a saucepan big enough to take all ingredients, lightly fry artichokes, onion and celery in half the butter, without allowing them to brown. Add water, stir and simmer on low heat for 20 minutes, then rub through a sieve or purée in a blender.

Melt remaining butter in a saucepan, stir in flour and cook together without allowing the roux to brown. Gradually blend in milk. Incorporate this sauce in the artichoke purée, reheat, season to taste. Just before serving blend in cream.

BRUSSELS SPROUTS SOUP

4 Servings

- ½ kg (1 lb) Brussels sprouts
- ½ kg (1 lb or 2½ cups) peeled thinly sliced potatoes
- 2 chopped onions
- ½ litre (1 pint or 2 cups) water
- salt and pepper

30 grs (1 oz or 2 tablespoons) butter
½ litre (1 pint or 2 cups) scalded milk

Trim, wash and drain sprouts. Cook sprouts, potatoes and onions in salted water for 20 minutes, or until tender, then rub through a sieve or purée in a blender. Put the purée back in the pan, reheat, incorporate butter, blending it in in small pieces. Stir in milk, season to taste with salt and pepper and serve.

CATALAN CREAM OF LANGOUSTINE SOUP

6 Servings

2 doz small langoustines (or prawns)
1 glass of white wine
1 onion
3 tomatoes
2 carrots
butter
3 tablespoons flour
fish stock
salt, pepper and saffron
2 yolks of eggs
3 tablespoons cream

Wash the langoustines and cook for 5 minutes in 2 litres (2 quarts) of boiling water with white wine added. Take the langoustines out of the water and keep the liquid. Remove the tails of the langoustines and keep. Crush the rest of the langoustines – shells and all – in a mortar into a smooth paste; or pass through a mincer. Chop the onion, the tomatoes, and the carrots very finely, mix with the langoustine paste. Melt 3 tablespoons of butter in a saucepan, sprinkle with flour, add the mixed ingredients. Fry until golden, slowly add the water in which the langoustines were boiled, stirring gently all the time. Cook for 1 hour, adding stock or water from time to time. Pass through a fine sieve, rubbing the vegetables, etc. through, season to taste with salt, pepper and saffron. Put in the langoustine tails. Cook for another 15 minutes. Blend yolk with cream. Away from heat stir yolks into soup and serve.

CREAM OF RICE SOUP

4 Servings

1 litre (1¾ pints or 4¼ cups) milk
1 small onion stuck with a clove
6–8 peppercorns
½ teaspoon salt
bouquet garni
45 grs (1½ oz or ¼ cup) ground rice
60 ml (½ gill or ¼ cup) cream

Reserve 120 ml (1 gill or ½ cup) milk for later use and heat the rest slowly. Add onion, peppercorns, salt and bouquet garni. Gently bring to the boil. Mix the rice with the reserved cold milk, blend well and stir the mixture into the pan. Reduce heat to low and simmer for 20 minutes.

Strain through a fine strainer into a heated soup tureen, stir in cream and serve.

RUSSIAN CREAM OF CUCUMBER SOUP

6 Servings

- 1½ kg (3 lb) cucumber
- 1½ litre (3 pints or 6 cups) tarragon consommé (p 107)
- 1–2 fresh black currant leaves
- 1 sprig chervil
- salt and pepper
- 4–5 tablespoons fresh cream
- 1 tablespoon chopped fresh dill or parsley

Peel the cucumber (reserve the peel) and with a small ball scoop out 30 cucumber balls. Keep these for garnish and chop the rest of the cucumbers.

Boil the cucumber balls in a little consommé for 8 minutes and drain. Add the liquid they were cooked in to the rest of the consommé with black currant leaves, chervil and cucumber peel. Bring to the boil, remove from heat and leave to infuse for 10 minutes, then strain. Put chopped cucumber into consommé, cook for 10 minutes, season to taste, then pass through a sieve or purée in a blender

If you intend to serve the soup hot, reheat, stir in cream, garnish with cucumber balls, sprinkle with dill and serve. Do not allow the soup to boil after adding cream. If you prefer it as a cold summer soup, add cream to the purée in the blender, cool and chill. Serve in individual bowls, garnished as above.

CALIFORNIAN CREAM OF PIMENTO SOUP

4 Servings

- 45 grs (1½ oz or 3 tablespoons) butter
- 1 small chopped onion
- 1 seeded chopped red pimento (sweet pepper)
- 1 seeded chopped green pimento
- 360 ml (¾ pint or 1½ cups) chicken stock
- 240 ml (½ pint or 1 cup) single cream or top of milk
- salt and pepper
- 90 grs (3 oz or ¾ cup) grated cheese

Heat butter in a saucepan and lightly fry onion and pimentos until soft. Stir in flour, cook without browning. Gradually add stock, stir to blend well. Simmer on low heat for 5 – 6 minutes.

Add cream, simmer stirring until the soup thickens, but do not allow it to boil. Season to taste with salt and pepper. Add cheese, stir until it melts and serve.

PENNSYLVANIA CREAM OF LENTIL SOUP

6 Servings

- 480 grs (1 lb or 2¼ cups) lentils
- 1¾ litres (3½ pints or 7 cups) stock
- 3 chopped stalks celery
- 1 chopped onion
- 120 grs (4 oz or ½ cup) single cream
- salt and pepper
- 2 tablespoons butter
- 6 tablespoons sherry
- 6 tablespoons whipped cream
- 2 tablespoons finely chopped parsley

Bring lentils to the boil in stock and simmer for 1 hour. Add celery and onion, continue to simmer for another 30 minutes. Rub through a sieve or purée in a blender. Put the lentil purée in a double saucepan and keep over simmering water. Add cream, season to taste and stir in butter.

Pour a tablespoon of sherry into each soup bowl, ladle in soup, put a rosette of whipped cream on top, sprinkle with parsley and serve.

MILK SOUPS

Milk soups are very nourishing, extremely simple to make and popular in the nursery. They should be cooked on a low heat, in a saucepan with a thick bottom.

You can ring the changes by using any of the following garnishes :

Cheese quenelles, klyotski, rice, fine vermicelli, soup nuts, almond dumplings, farfel, etc. Recipes for all these can be found under garnishes.

RUSSIAN MILK SOUP WITH NOODLES

6 Servings

- 120 grs (4 oz) home-made noodles (p 46)
- 1 litre (2 pints or 4 cups) milk
- ½ teaspoon salt
- 1 teaspoon sugar
- 1 tablespoon butter

Prepare the noodles. Bring milk to the boil, add noodles, salt and sugar. Simmer for 15 minutes. Before serving add butter. This soup is also very good made with vermicelli.

MILK SOUP WITH POTATO DUMPLINGS

6 Servings

- 1 litre (2 pints or 4 cups) milk
- 1 tablespoon butter
- potato dumplings (p 147)
- salt

Bring milk to the boil. Drop dumplings into hot milk. Simmer on the lowest possible heat for 10 minutes, season with salt to taste, add a little butter and serve.

Milk soups can also be made with almond dumplings or soup nuts.

BELGIAN CHICORY MILK SOUP

6 Servings

- ½ kg (1 lb or 2 cups) finely chopped chicory
- 2 finely chopped leeks, white portion only
- 3 peeled thinly sliced potatoes
- 6 tablespoons butter
- 1½ litres (3 pints or 6 cups) scalded milk
- salt and pepper

In a big saucepan lightly fry chicory, leeks and potatoes in butter without allowing the vegetables to brown. Add milk, season to taste, simmer very gently for 35–40 minutes. Serve with dry toast.

COLD SOUPS

TARRAGON CONSOMMÉ

Prepare, clarify and strain consommé as usual. 5–6 minutes before serving add 2–3 tablespoons fresh tarragon leaves. Keep hot but do not allow to boil. Strain, chill and serve.

COLD CONSOMMÉ MADRID STYLE

Cook the chicken consommé as described (p. 85). When you clarify it, add ¼ litre (½ pint or 1 cup) raw tomato pulp, rubbed through a sieve. Strain and chill. Serve cold with a tablespoon of sweet pepper diced, simmered in a little stock and cooled, for every serving.

COLD CONSOMMÉ WITH WINE

Prepare, clarify and strain consommé as described. Allow to cool, then add sherry, port, Madeira or any similar wine. Allow 1 dcl (1 gill or ½ cup) wine to a litre (1 quart) of consommé. Chill and serve.

VICHYSSOISE I

4–6 Servings

60 grs (2 oz or 4 tablespoons) unsalted butter
3–4 sliced leeks, white part only
1 onion sliced
5 medium-sized potatoes, peeled and sliced finely
1½ litres (1½ quarts) chicken stock
1 dcl (1 gill or ½ cup) double cream
salt and pepper
pinch nutmeg
1–1½ tablespoons chopped chives

Heat butter in a saucepan and lightly fry leeks and onion stirring with a wooden spoon. Add potatoes and cook together for 2 – 3 minutes. Add stock and simmer for 40 minutes. Rub through a fine sieve or pass through a food mill and allow to cool.

When cold, blend in cream, season to taste with salt, pepper and nutmeg. Chill, serve cold sprinkled with chopped chives.

VICHYSSOISE II

As above but instead of using 5 potatoes, use 3 potatoes and 3 carrots. Use 2 carrots in cooking and leave 1 grated carrot raw for last minute garnish. Cook as described, omitting chives. Chill the Vichyssoise, ladle out into individual cups, sprinkle with raw grated carrot and serve. Try also Vichyssoise made only of carrots and using stock and unsweetened orange juice in equal proportions.

BLOODY MARY SOUP

4–6 Servings

1 litre (2 pints or 4 cups) chilled tomato juice
1 teaspoon sugar
salt and pepper to taste
2 teaspoons Worcester sauce
½ teaspoon Tabasco sauce
2 tablespoons fresh lime (or lemon) juice
120 ml (4 oz or ½ cup) vodka
120 ml (4 oz or ½ cup) sour cream (optional)

Mix all ingredients adding them in the order listed. Chill and serve in cups. If you get generous with the vodka, you will turn your soup into a straight aperitif.

COLD JELLIED CONSOMMÉ WITH CAVIAR

This makes an excellent appetizer and first course on a hot day.

6 Servings

1 litre (2 pints or 4 cups) strong consommé (p 85)
2 tablespoons unflavoured gelatine (optional)
120 ml (4 oz or ½ cup) port or sherry
3 tablespoons black or red caviar

If your consommé was based on stock made with a veal knuckle, it should set without any outside help. If not, strengthen with gelatine.

Soften gelatine in ½ cup cold consommé, allow to dissolve over hot water, without contact with direct heat. Mix with the rest of consommé. Add port or sherry, stir and chill. Just before serving put half a tablespoon of caviar in the bottom of each chilled cup. Stir the consommé with a knife, ladle into cups and serve.

COLD JELLIED CONSOMMÉ WITH AVOCADO

Prepare consommé as above. Garnish with avocado cut in small dice.

JEWISH SOUR CREAM BORSCH (COLD)

8 Servings

This version of borsch is served cold and, because no meat is used in the recipe, it has a dressing of sour cream, which is added just before serving. Left-over borsch should be poured into a screw top jar and kept in the refrigerator.

- 3–4 large beetroots
- 2½ litres (2½ quarts) water
- 2 carrots
- ½ parsnip
- 2 stalks celery
- 2 large onions
- 1 finely chopped clove garlic
- 480 gr (1 lb or 2 cups) peeled fresh or tinned tomatoes
- 1 tablespoon sugar
- 1½–2 teaspoons salt
- 1 tablespoon wine vinegar
- 1 bay leaf
- ½ teaspoon ground black pepper
- 5–6 whole Allspice seeds
- 3 tablespoons dry white wine
- 2 dcl (½ pint or 1 cup) sour cream
- lemon or cucumber slices for garnish

Scrub, peel and cut up beetroot, reserving one for subsequent colouring. Put in a saucepan with water, bring to the boil, cover and simmer for 1 hour. Meanwhile, cut up all the other vegetables and add to pan with sugar, salt, vinegar, bay leaf, pepper and Allspice. Cook for a further 45–60 minutes, until beetroot is tender. Put the vegetables with a cup of the soup through a blender until smooth, or rub through a sieve. Strain the soup into a bowl, add the blended vegetables to it, check seasoning and colour. If necessary, add some of the reserved beetroot, as described in recipe on page 27. Add wine, stir, cover and allow to cool completely, then chill, preferably overnight.

Serve in individual soup bowls, topped with a dollop of sour cream and garnished with a slice of lemon or a few thin slices of fresh cucumber.

ANDALUSIAN GAZPACHO

These cold soups are delicious and particularly refreshing on a hot summer evening. In Spain they are often served with bread which is dunked into the gazpacho.

4–6 Servings

- 1 clove peeled garlic
- 1 sliced onion
- 2–3 tablespoons oil
- 1–2 tablespoons vinegar
- 6 slices of bread with crusts cut off
- ¼ litre (½ pint or 1 cup) iced water
- 1 large tin tomato juice
- salt and pepper

For garnish

- 3 large peeled, seeded, diced tomatoes
- 1 seeded, diced green pimento
- 1 peeled, diced cucumber
- 2–3 chopped hard-boiled eggs
- diced croûtons
- 12 ice cubes

Crush the garlic. Add onion sprinkle with 1 tablespoon oil and the vinegar. Leave to stand for ½ hour. Soak bread in water. Pound the garlic and onion with soaked bread, or put through a blender, using the water in which the bread was soaked and tomato juice, to dilute the mixture. Season with salt and pepper to taste and drop by drop whisk in the remaining oil. Chill in refrigerator.

Put the garnish of tomatoes, pimento, cucumber, chopped eggs and croûtons in separate dishes.

Add ice cubes to gazpacho and serve with the garnishes.

MALAGA GAZPACHO

4 Servings

- 90 grs (3 oz) white bread
- water
- 6 tablespoons olive oil
- 4 tablespoons chopped blanched almonds
- 2 tablespoons vinegar
- 1 pounded clove garlic
- salt
- 10–12 ice cubes
- parsley

Remove crusts and dice the bread. Put in a bowl, add enough water to soak. Drain bread and pass through a blender with ¼ litre (½ pint or 1 cup) cold water, olive oil, almonds, vinegar, garlic and salt. As soon as the mixture is smooth, add another ½ litre (1 pint or 2 cups) water and blend thoroughly. If you have one of those small blenders, pass the ingredients through it in two lots; if a blender is not available the ingredients will have to be rubbed through a sieve. Pour into a tureen and chill the gazpacho.

Before serving, add ice cubes. Garnish with parsley and serve with croûtons fried in oil (p. 144).

GAZPACHO MARINA

6 Servings

- 3 onions
- 1 kg (2 lb or 4 cups) ripe red peeled tomatoes
- 1 long French loaf sliced
- 1 dcl (1 gill or ½ cup) oil
- 2 doz peeled blanched almonds
- 1 tablespoon salt
- 2 tablespoons vinegar
- 1 cucumber
- 12 ice cubes

Peel and pass the onions, cucumber and tomatoes through a mincer, collecting all the juice. Sieve these vegetables and together with their juice, mix with the sliced bread. Add oil and stir until the mixture becomes light and creamy. Pound the almonds in a mortar, add slowly 250 ml (½ pint or 1 cup) of water, mixing first into a paste, then into a milky liquid. Strain through a sieve and pour in the salad bowl. Season with salt and vinegar, add the ice cubes, mix and serve. This gazpacho must have the consistency of pease-pudding. If it is too thick, add iced water before serving.

ALBA AVOCADO SOUP

This is a very interesting variation of avocado soup, a Cuban speciality, with white rum. Once your stock is ready, there is no cooking to be done.

4 Servings

- pulp of 1 ripe avocado
- ½ litre (1 pint or 2 cups) chicken consommé (p 85)
- ¼ litre (½ pint or 1 cup) single cream
- 2 tablespoons white rum
- ½ teaspoon curry powder (see garam-masala (p 150)
- ½ teaspoon salt
- freshly ground pepper
- juice of 1 lime
- 1 tablespoon finely chopped chives

Combine all ingredients, except chives, and purée in a blender; if a blender is not available the ingredients will have to be rubbed through a sieve. Chill thoroughly. Ladle into chilled consommé cups, sprinkle with chives and serve.

AVOCADO GAZPACHO

This is another cold avocado soup with mixed vegetables. It

makes a delicious and refreshing summer starter and is a speciality of the Sheraton Hotel in Tel-Aviv.

6 Servings

- 480 grs (1 lb or 2 cups) avocado flesh
- 2 sliced, medium-sized onions
- 240 ml (8 oz or 1 cup) dry white wine
- juice of 1 lemon
- 240 ml (8 oz or 1 cup) iced water
- 1 teaspoon sugar
- 1 teaspoon salt
- black pepper

for garnish:

- 60 grs (2 oz or ¼ cup) peeled, diced tomatoes
- 60 grs (2 oz or ¼ cup) seeded, diced green pepper
- 60 grs (2 oz or ¼ cup) diced cucumber

Pass the avocado and onions through a blender with wine, lemon juice and water; if a blender is not available the ingredients will have to be rubbed through a sieve. Add sugar, season to taste with salt and pepper, transfer to a bowl and chill.

Make sure tomatoes, peppers and cucumber are cut in uniform small dice. Mix this garnish and chill.

Serve the gazpacho iced, in individual bowls, topped with a portion of mixed, diced vegetables.

MELON SOUP

6 Servings

- 1 melon
- 1 litre (1 quart) chicken stock
- ½ bottle dry white wine
- salt and pepper
- pinch mace

Cut the melon, discard seeds, scoop out some of the flesh with a ball scoop and reserve 18 of these for garnish. Keep them in a refrigerator. Dice the rest of the melon, keeping all the juice which flows out.

Heat the stock with the wine, add seasoning, bring to the boil. Put in diced melon flesh and its juice, cook over gentle heat for 20 minutes. Pass the whole of the soup through a sieve, or a blender, cool and chill. Garnish with melon balls and serve.

VEGETABLE OKROSHKA

This is a delicious summer soup popular throughout all parts of Russia.

4–5 Servings

- 1 litre (2 pints or 4 cups) kvas (p 22)
- 1 large cooked beetroot

1 cooked carrot
1 cucumber
1–2 boiled potatoes
30 grs (1 oz) spring onions
1 teaspoon salt
2 hard-boiled eggs
½ teaspoon dry mustard
2 tablespoons sour cream
1 teaspoon sugar
sprig of dill (or parsley)
ice cubes

Uncork kvas. Dice the beetroot, carrot, cucumber and potatoes. Chop the spring onions finely, season with salt and press the salt into the onions with a fork to release juices. Halve the eggs, separate the yolks from the whites and chop the whites finely.

Blend the yolks with the mustard. Combine the crushed spring onions with potatoes, yolks, sour cream, sugar, chopped whites of egg and a little salt to taste. Mix well, add the kvas gradually, put in beetroot, cucumber and carrot, sprinkle with chopped dill or parsley and serve with ice cubes.

Other cooked vegetables may be used instead of carrots and beetroot – for instance young turnips or cauliflowers – but cucumber is absolutely essential.

MEAT OKROSHKA

4–5 Servings

1 litre (1 quart) kvas (p 22)
120 grs (¼ lb) cooked beef
120 grs (¼ lb) boiled ham, cut thick
120 grs (¼ lb) cooked tongue or any meat or game leftovers – bits of roast chicken, duck lamb, veal, anything so long as it is not fat)
1 fresh cucumber
1 salted cucumber (optional)
30 gr (1 oz) spring onions
sprig of dill (or parsley)
pinch of tarragon
2 hard-boiled eggs
1 teaspoon made mustard
1 teaspoon salt
1 teaspoon sugar
120 ml (4 oz or ½ cup) sour cream
ice cubes

Uncork kvas. Dice all the cooked meats and the cucumber. Chop the spring onions, the dill and tarragon. Separate the whites from the yolks and chop the whites. Put the yolks in a tureen, add mustard, salt sugar and sour cream. Stir.

Gradually pour in the kvas, add all the other ingredients, and serve with coarsely crushed ice.

LATVIAN BREAD SOUP

4 Servings

480 grs (1 lb) unsalted rye bread
1½ litres (1½ quarts) boiling water
30 grs (1 oz or 3 tablespoons) seedless raisins
30 grs (1 oz or 3 tablespoons) currants

- 120 grs (4 oz or 1¼ cups) dried apple slices
- 180 grs (6 oz or 1½ cups) cranberries
- 2 tablespoons sugar
- pinch cinnamon
- 120 ml (4 oz or ½ cup) cream for whipping

Cut the bread into slices and dry in the oven to make rusks. Put in a bowl, cover with boiling water and leave to swell. Rub through a sieve into a saucepan, with all the liquid. Add raisins, currants and apples. Rub cranberries through a sieve and add to soup.

Sprinkle in sugar and cinnamon, bring to the boil, then simmer for 10 minutes.

Remove from heat, cool and chill. Serve cold with a topping of whipped cream.

UKRAINIAN CUCUMBER AND BEETROOT SOUP

6 Servings

- ½ kg (1 lb) beets with green tops
- ½ kg (1 lb) cucumber
- 1 carrot
- 4–5 spring onions
- 1 litre (2 pints or 4 cups) buttermilk
- 1 tablespoon chopped dill (or parsley)
- salt and pepper
- 3 hard-boiled eggs
- 1 carton sour cream

Wash the beets, dry, bake, peel and dice.

Cook the beet tops in a little salted water, drain well and chop. Peel and dice cucumber. Grate carrot. Chop spring onions.

Mix buttermilk, beetroot and beet tops, cucumber, carrot and onions. Sprinkle with dill and season to taste. Chill.

Decant into individual bowls. Garnish with quarters of hard-boiled egg, decorate with a swirl of sour cream and serve.

COLD CREAM OF ARTICHOKE SOUP

6 Servings

- ½ litre (1 pint or 2 cups) creamy Béchamel (p 22)
- ½ litre (1 pint or 2 cups) chicken consommé (p 85)
- 6 artichoke hearts
- salt and pepper

Dilute Béchamel with consommé.

Mash half the artichoke hearts and dice the rest for garnish. Blend mashed artichoke hearts with consommé and Béchamel. Season to taste. Mix well. Chill and serve with a portion of diced artichoke heart in each plate.

YEMENITE YOGHURT SOUP

This is reputed by the Yemenites to be a health-giving summer soup. It is certainly a refreshing one and has an added advantage – it requires no cooking.

4 Servings

- 240 grs (8 oz or 1 cup) peeled diced cucumber
- 1 clove garlic
- 1 tablespoon vinegar
- ½ litre (1 pint or 2 cups) yoghurt
- salt
- 1 tablespoon olive oil
- 1 tablespoon fresh chopped mint

Put the cucumbers in a dish, sprinkle with salt and leave for 30 minutes.

Slice garlic and rub with it a bowl big enough to take all the ingredients. Sprinkle in vinegar and rinse the bowl with it. Spoon yoghurt into this vinegar and garlic flavoured bowl and stir to thin down, adding 2–3 tablespoons of water, if necessary.

Drain cucumbers, add to yoghurt, mix and chill. Blend in olive oil, a few drops at a time, chill, sprinkle with mint and serve.

CHILLED CREAM OF PARSLEY SOUP

6 Servings

- large bunch parsley
- ¾ litres (1½ pints or 3 cups) consommé (p 85)
- 2 eggs
- ½ litre (1 pint or 2 cups) single cream
- salt
- cayenne pepper
- 6 tablespoons whipped cream

Wash parsley, reserve six short-stemmed sprigs for garnishing and chop the rest finely or pass through a parsley mill.

Bring consommé to the boil, add parsley, simmer for 20–25 minutes, strain, and pour soup into a double boiler. Keep over gently simmering water.

Beat eggs with single cream, stir into soup and season to taste with salt and cayenne pepper. Continue to simmer until the soup thickens. Check seasoning, cool and chill.

To serve, ladle into chilled consommé cups.

Whip the cream with a pinch of salt, put a dollop of this slightly salty whipped cream on top and decorate with a sprig of parsley

SENEGALESE CHILLED CREAM OF CHICKEN SOUP

6 Servings

- 1¼ litres (2½ pints or 5 cups) chicken stock (p 18)
- 3 raw yolks

240 ml (½ pint or 1 cup) double cream
2 teaspoons garam-masala (p 150)
salt
pinch cayenne pepper
120 grs (4 oz or ½ cup) cooked breast of chicken
2 tablespoons finely chopped parsley

Scald the stock and pour into the top of a double saucepan. Keep over simmering water.

Beat eggs with cream, garam-masala, salt and cayenne pepper and add to stock. Simmer stirring until the soup thickens.

Remove from heat, check seasoning, cool and chill. Dice breast of chicken and stir into the soup. Spoon into chilled cups, sprinkle with parsley and serve.

This soup is sometimes garnished with unpeeled diced red apple.

SCANDINAVIAN DILL SOUP (CHILLED)

The liquid for this soup is a mixture of sour cream and potato water. The potatoes themselves can be mashed and used another day. See American Congress Bean Soup.

4 Servings
480 grs (1 lb or 2½ cups) raw diced potatoes
salt and pepper
water
1½ tablespoons flour
360 ml (¾ pint or 1½ cup) scalded sour cream
1 large bunch dill
2 raw yolks
dash nutmeg

Cook potatoes in boiling salted water to give you ½ litre (1 pint or 2 cups) potato water. Simmer potatoes until tender and drain off potato water into a saucepan. Heat gently.

Dilute flour with 3 tablespoons cold water.

Stir a third of the sour cream into soup, followed by a tablespoon of water and flour mixture. Continue until 240 ml (½ pint or 1 cup) of sour cream and all the flour and water have been blended in.

Wash dill, reserve a few sprigs for garnishing and chop the rest finely or put through a mill. Add to soup, bring to the boil, simmer for 3–4 minutes.

Beat yolks with remaining scalded sour cream and stir into the soup. Bring to the boil, season to taste with salt and pepper, add nutmeg, stir and remove from heat. Cool, then chill. Serve in individual consommé cups garnished with little sprigs of dill.

FREDA KOBLICK'S AMERICAN CHILLED ORANGE AND TOMATO SOUP

4 Servings

- ½ litre (1 pint or 2 cups) strained orange juice
- ½ litre (1 pint or 2 cups) tomato juice
- 120 ml (4 oz or ½ cup) dry white wine
- juice of ½ lemon
- 1 teaspoon sugar
- salt
- cayenne pepper
- 1 tablespoon finely chopped parsley

Blend orange juice with tomato juice, wine and lemon juice. Add sugar, season to taste with salt and cayenne pepper. Chill and serve sprinkled with parsley.

Fruit Soups

HOT CHERRY SOUP

6–8 Servings

- 600 grs ($1\frac{1}{4}$ lb or 3 cups) stoned, sweet cherries
- 2 litre (2 quarts) water
- 1 stick cinnamon
- 1 lemon, thinly sliced
- 120 grs (4 oz or $\frac{1}{2}$ cup) sugar
- 120 ml (4 oz or $\frac{1}{2}$ cup) sweet white wine
- $1\frac{1}{2}$ tablespoons cornflour
- rusks

Put half the cherries with water into a pan, bring to the boil and simmer until tender. Strain into another pan, rubbing the cherry flesh through. Put back to heat. Add cinnamon, lemon slices and the rest of the cherries. Simmer for 5 minutes. Sprinkle in sugar, add wine, simmer until sugar is dissolved.

Dilute cornflour with 2 tablespoons water and stir into the soup. As soon as the soup thickens slightly, remove from heat.

Serve rusks separately. Cherry soup can also be served chilled.

KARELIAN RHUBARB SOUP

This soup can be served hot or cold. In Finland it is usually served hot, with rusks.

6 Servings

- 1 kg (2 lb) rhubarb
- 2 litres (2 quarts) water
- 1 stick cinnamon
- 2–3 slices lemon
- 240 grs (8 oz or 1 cup) sugar
- 2 tablespoons cornflour
- 1 raw yolk
- 120 ml (4 oz or $\frac{1}{2}$ cup) double cream

Wash rhubarb, strip off any strings, cut and simmer in water until tender. Rub through a sieve with all its liquid, or pass through a blender. Return to saucepan, add cinnamon, lemon and sugar. Stir to dissolve sugar completely, simmer for 7–8 minutes. Remove cinnamon and lemon.

Dilute cornflour with 3 tablespoons cold water and blend into the hot soup. Simmer, stirring, for 3–4 minutes, until the soup thickens. Remove from heat.

Whisk yolk with cream, stir into the soup and serve.

DANISH ELDERBERRY SOUP

6 Servings

750 grs (1½ lbs or 3 cups) ripe elderberries
1½ litre (3 pints or 6 cups) water
sugar
grated rind of ½ lemon
pinch of cinnamon
1½ tablespoons cornflour

De-stalk the berries, wash, drain, put in a pan with water. Bring to the boil, simmer gently until the berries become soft and yield up their juice. Press through a fine sieve. Return elderberry purée and all liquid to pan with lemon rind, cinnamon and sugar to taste. Dissolve cornflour in 3 tablespoons cold water, blend into the soup, simmer stirring until the soup thickens and serve.

SCANDINAVIAN PRUNE SOUP

6 Servings

2 litres (2 quarts) water
6 tablespoons sago
240 grs (8 oz or 1 cup) stoned prunes
pinch cinnamon
240 ml (½ pint or 1 cup) cranberry or other red fruit juice
sugar to taste
3 tablespoons slivered almonds

Cook the sago in boiling water, stirring, for 5 minutes. Add prunes and simmer until they are soft. Add cinnamon, fruit juice and sugar to taste. Simmer for 30 minutes. Sprinkle in almonds and serve hot or cold.

FREDA KOBLICK'S CALIFORNIAN FRUIT AND WINE SOUP

6 Servings

180 grs (6 oz or ¾ cup) sugar
1 tablespoon cornflour
240 ml (8 oz or 1 cup) water
5 cm (2 inch) stick cinnamon
pinch nutmeg
pinch mace
6 thin slices of lemon
1 bottle red or rosé wine
750 grs (1½ lb or 3 cups) raspberries (or strawberries)

Mix sugar with cornflour, dilute with water and put to heat. Simmer stirring constantly until the syrup thickens. Add the rest of the ingredients in the order listed, simmer for 3 minutes. Remove cinnamon stick. Serve hot or chilled.

SWEDISH BLUEBERRY SOUP WITH ALMOND DUMPLINGS

6 Servings

1 kg (2 lb or 4 cups) blueberries
2 litres (2 quarts) water
90 grs (3 oz or 6 tablespoons) sugar
3 tablespoons cornflour
almond dumplings (p 147)

Cook the blueberries in water until soft. Strain, rub through a sieve or pass through a blender. Return to pan, heat, add sugar and simmer on low heat until it dissolves.

Dissolve cornflour with 3 tablespoons cold water, stir into the pan, simmer until the soup thickens.

Poach the dumplings separately. Drain, add to blueberry soup and serve.

COLD BLUEBERRY SOUP

Follow above recipe, omit dumplings. Chill the soup and serve with a topping of whipped cream.

RUSSIAN CRANBERRY AND APPLE SOUP

6 Servings

375 grs (12 oz or 3 cups) cranberries
1 litre (1 quart) boiling water
240 grs (½ lb) cooking apples
4–6 tablespoons sugar (or to taste)
1 tablespoon cornflour
3 tablespoons cold water
120 ml (4 oz or ½ cup) sour cream

Wash and mash cranberries in a saucepan. Pour in boiling water, stir, cover and leave to stand for 15 minutes. Strain into a saucepan, pressing out all the juice. Add sugar and stir to dissolve.

Peel, core and slice apples. Add to cranberry juice, gently bring to the boil. Simmer for 2–3 minutes. Mix cornflour with cold water and stir into the soup. Remove from heat, chill and serve with sour cream.

CRIMEAN CURRANT AND PEACH SOUP

6 Servings

375 grs (12 oz or 3 cups) red or blackcurrants
1 litre (1 quart) boiling water
240 grs (½ lb) peaches

4–6 tablespoons sugar (or to taste)
1 tablespoon cornflour
3 tablespoons cold water
120 ml (4 oz or ½ cup) sour cream

Prepare as described in recipe for Cranberry and Apple Soup. Dip the peaches in hot water for a moment to loosen skins, peel and stone before slicing.

CALIFORNIAN STRAWBERRY SOUP

6 Servings

½ kg (1 lb or 3 cups) strawberries
½ litre (1 pint or 2 cups) red wine
¼ litre (½ pint or 1 cup) water
60 grs (2 oz or ¼ cup) sugar
pinch salt
3 tablespoons arrowroot
120 ml (4 oz or ½ cup) single cream

Wash and hull strawberries and put in a saucepan with red wine and water. Bring to the boil, add sugar and salt, simmer until sugar is dissolved, stirring from time to time.

Dilute arrowroot with 4 tablespoons cold water and stir the mixture into hot soup. Reheat stirring until the soup thickens. Remove from heat, chill and serve topped with cream.

ARMENIAN APRICOT AND RICE SOUP

4 Servings

½ kg (1 lb) fresh apricots
1 litre (1 quart) water
4 tablespoons sugar
1 tablespoon cornflour
3 tablespoons cold water
3 tablespoons cold cooked rice
4 tablespoons whipped cream

Wash, halve and stone the apricots. Bring to the boil, simmer for 10 minutes and rub through a sieve or pass through a blender with the liquid in which they were cooked. Add sugar, heat to boiling point. Dilute cornflour with cold water and stir into the soup. Remove from heat, cool, add rice and chill. Serve cold with a topping of whipped cream.

FINNISH BILBERRY SOUP

4 Servings

500 grs (1 lb or 2 cups) bilberries (or other berries)
1 litre (2 pints or 4 cups) water
120 grs (4 oz or ½ cup) sugar
2½ tablespoons potato flour
120 ml (4 oz or ½ cup) whipped cream

Pick over the berries, bring to the boil in water. As soon as they start to burst, add sugar, simmer until the sugar dissolves. Mix potato flour with 2 tablespoons of cold water, stir into the soup, simmer until it thickens and remove from heat. Cool, chill and serve with a topping of whipped cream.

MIXED FRUIT SOUP

6 Servings

2 apples
2 pears
juice of 1 lemon
1 peach
150 grs (5 oz or about 1 cup) hulled strawberries
750 ml ($\frac{3}{4}$ quart or $3\frac{1}{4}$ cups) water
2 tablespoons sugar (or to taste)
480 ml (1 pint or 2 cups) orange juice
$1\frac{1}{2}$ tablespoons cornflour
120 ml (4 oz or $\frac{1}{2}$ cup) dry white wine
small carton soured cream
fresh mint

Peel and core apples and pears and dip in lemon juice to prevent discoloration. Dip peach into boiling water for a few seconds, skin it and remove stone. Dice apples, pears and peach. Leave small strawberries whole, slice large ones. Put water and sugar to boil, add fruit and simmer for 4–5 minutes. Add orange juice.

Dilute cornflour with 2 tablespoons cold water and whatever is left of the lemon juice, and stir into the soup. Simmer gently, for a couple of minutes and remove from heat. Allow to cool, then chill.

Just before serving, add wine. Serve in individual bowls, with a dollop of sour cream on top and decorate with fresh mint.

ISRAELI APPLE AND RED WINE SOUP

4 Servings

1 kg (2 lb or 6 medium-sized) cooking apples
60 grs (2 oz or 4 tablespoons) butter
120 ml (4 oz or $\frac{1}{2}$ cup) water
pinch nutmeg
$\frac{1}{2}$ teaspoon lemon rind
lemon juice
1 bottle red wine (not too dry)
120 ml (4 oz or $\frac{1}{2}$ cup) sour cream

Peel core and slice the apples. Melt butter in a pan, add apples, cook gently, then add water and simmer until apples are quite soft. Add nutmeg, lemon rind and a dash of lemon juice, rub through a sieve or pass through a blender for perfect smoothness, and cool.

Dilute with red wine, add 2–3 tablespoons lemon juice to sharpen the soup.

If you are going to serve it hot, reheat, stir in sour cream and serve. If it is to be served cold, stir in sour cream without reheating, chill.

Special Soups

AVGOLEMONO SOUP

4–6 Servings

- $1\frac{1}{2}$ litre (3 pints or 6 cups) fish or light meat stock
- 90 grs (3 oz or 6 tablespoons) uncooked rice
- salt and pepper
- 3 eggs
- juice of 1–2 lemons

Bring stock to the boil, throw in rice, season to taste and cook for 15 minutes.

Beat the eggs with lemon juice until frothy, gradually dilute with a cup of hot stock, blending it in slowly. Remove the rice soup from heat, stir in egg and lemon mixture and serve at once. On no account allow the soup to boil after adding the egg and lemon sauce.

MAYONNAISE SOUP

This delicious soup probably originates in Minorca, which also gave us the famous sauce. People who are used to seeing mayonnaise on the menus spelled the French way, may not realise that it is, in fact, a Spanish invention. It was first introduced into France after the capture of the port of Mahon in Minorca by the French in 1757. It takes its Spanish name mahonesa from Mahon.

6 Servings

- 180 grs (6 oz) bread
- 1 litre (1 quart) water
- 2 tablespoons oil
- 180 grs (6 oz) hake (or similar fish)
- 240 grs (8 oz or 1 cup) peeled, thinly sliced potatoes
- salt and pepper
- garlic-flavoured mayonnaise

Slice the bread, put in a pan with water and slowly bring to the boil. Heat the oil and lightly fry the fish, remove from heat. Skin and bone the fish, slice and add to the bread. Stir, add potatoes, season to taste. Simmer for 45–50 minutes. Then rub through a sieve and whisk until smooth, or put the soup through a blender. Keep hot.

Make the mayonnaise. Be sure to flavour it with garlic. To do this, pound a peeled clove of garlic into paste with a tiny pinch of salt. Add this mixture to a raw yolk in the bowl in which you plan to make the sauce. Blend well and proceed to make the sauce as usual (p. 23).

When the mayonnaise is ready, pour into a heated tureen, stir the sauce into it and serve at once.

DANISH BUTTERMILK SOUP

4–6 Servings

- 2 tablespoons butter
- 2 tablespoons flour
- 1 litre (2 pints or 4 cups) buttermilk
- ½ teaspoon grated lemon rind
- 30 grs (1 oz or 3 tablespoons) seedless raisins
- 1½ tablespoons blanched roughly chopped almonds
- sugar
- 4–6 slices lemon

In a saucepan heat butter, stir in flour and cook together without allowing the mixture to brown. Add buttermilk, stirring it in a little at a time. Add lemon rind, simmer for 5 minutes. Add raisins, almonds and sugar to taste, and serve.

This soup looks particularly attractive served in a dark-glazed bowl with semi-circular lemon slices set upright on the top.

SPANISH GARLIC SOUP

6 Servings

- 3 tablespoons oil
- 4 cloves garlic
- 180 grs (6 oz) stale bread
- pinch paprika
- 1½ litre (1½ quarts) salted water
- 2–3 tablespoons milk

Heat oil and fry garlic until golden. Cut bread into very thin slices, fry with the garlic, remove and put in an oven-proof tureen.

Stir paprika into oil, remove from heat as soon as it is blended in. Bring salted water to the boil, pour over bread slices, cover and leave to stand for 5 minutes. Remove garlic and discard. Mix garlic-flavoured oil with a little milk, add to soup, stir well. Put in a hot oven for 5–6 minutes to give the bread, which floats up to the surface, a nice, crusty, brown top.

SPANISH GARLIC SOUP WITH BEATEN EGG

6 Servings

Prepare garlic soup as described, but after frying the bread, remove garlic from pan and fry 150 grs (5 ozs or 1 cup) peeled chopped tomatoes. Remove from heat, add 2 beaten eggs and 2–3 tablespoons milk, blend well and pour the mixture into the soup.

Check seasoning, add a little freshly ground black pepper, stir well and serve. This makes a satisfying and delicious soup.

SPANISH GARLIC SOUP WITH POACHED EGGS

6 Servings

Prepare garlic soup as described. Just before serving, add a lightly poached, trimmed egg to each plate.

AMERICAN CHEESE AND BEER SOUP

6 Servings

- 30 grs (1 oz or 2 tablespoons) butter
- 30 grs (1 oz or 4 tablespoons) flour
- ¾ litre (1½ pints or 3 cups) hot chicken stock
- 2 tablespoons finely chopped onion
- 3 tablespoons finely chopped carrot
- 2 tablespoons finely chopped celery
- 1½ tablespoons finely chopped parsley
- 1 tablespoon finely chopped chives
- 120 grs (4 oz or 1 cup) grated cheese
- ½ litre (1 pint or 2 cups) beer
- salt and pepper
- popcorn (optional)

In a saucepan melt butter, stir in flour and cook a pale golden roux, stirring all the time. Gradually blend in stock, bring to the boil.

Add onion, carrot, celery, parsley and chives. Simmer for 15 minutes. Add cheese, simmer for 5 minutes.

Warm the beer and add to soup. Heat to boiling point, season to taste and serve.

Popcorn is the garnish recommended for this soup.

Personally, I prefer bread or potato croûtons (p. 144) well drained and sprinkled with fine salt.

AUSTRIAN KUMMEL SOUP WITH PASTA

6 Servings

- 60 grs (2 oz or 4 tablespoons) butter
- $1\frac{1}{2}$ tablespoons flour
- 1 teaspoon caraway seeds
- 750 ml ($1\frac{1}{2}$ pints or $3\frac{1}{4}$ cups) boiling water
- 180 grs (6 oz or $1\frac{1}{2}$ cups) noodles, broken spaghetti or other pasta
- salt and pepper

In a saucepan heat butter and stir in flour. Cook, stirring until the roux is pale golden. Sprinkle in caraway seeds, cook for 1 minute. Dilute with boiling water, adding it a little at a time and stirring well. Bring to the boil, simmer for 20–25 minutes.

Cook the pasta separately in salted boiling water for 10 minutes.

Strain the soup through a muslin bag to catch all the seeds. Drain the pasta and add to soup. Bring to the boil, season to taste and serve.

AUSTRIAN BEER SOUP

6 Servings

- 1 litre (2 pints or $4\frac{1}{4}$ cups) beer
- 6 raw yolks
- 180 grs (6 oz or $\frac{3}{4}$ cup) sugar
- 120 ml (4 oz $\frac{1}{2}$ cup) single cream
- pinch cinnamon

Pour the beer into a double saucepan and start heating gently. Whisk yolks, add sugar and mix well. Stir in cream.

Reduce the heat so that the soup is cooked over barely simmering water. Add yolk and cream mixture to beer. Simmer very gently stirring all the time until the soup thickens. Sprinkle with cinnamon and serve.

CHAWAN-MUSHI

This is, perhaps, the most famous of Japanese custard soups. Owing to the method of preparation this soup is frequently included under steamed dishes on menus in Japanese restaurants.

4 Servings

- 125 grs (4 oz or $\frac{1}{2}$ cup) sliced chicken
- shoyu
- 60 grs (2 oz) dried mushrooms
- 12 gingko nuts
- 1 litre (2 pints or 4 cups) *dashi* (see p 21)
- salt
- Aji-no-Moto
- 4 eggs
- $\frac{1}{2}$ kamaboko fish paste
- 12 trefoils (or water cress)
- 2 tiger-lily bulbs
- 1 tablespoon vinegar
- 8 peeled shrimps or prawns
- 2 thin slices lemon

Sprinkle chicken with 1 tablespoon shoyu and leave to stand for 15 minutes. Soak mushrooms in cold water for 10 minutes to soften; trim off stalks. Shell and boil gingko nuts to remove outer layer of flesh. Heat dashi, season with salt, shoyu and Aji-no-Moto. Leave to cool.

Beat eggs, whisk into cold dashi, and strain.

Cut kamaboko into neat slices diagonally. Tie trefoils as described in recipe for Trefoil and Triangular Egg Soup (see p. 94), dip into hot water for a second, trim ends to a uniform length.

Peel tiger-lily bulbs, put into a pan with ½ litre (1 pint or 2 cups) water and the vinegar, bring to the boil, strain and slice.

Divide all ingredients, including shrimps, equally in 4 bowls, decorate with trefoil bouquets, add half a slice of lemon to each, fill with egg and dashi mixture, cover the bowls, put in a steamer (or bain-marie) and steam until set (15–20 minutes). Serve in the same covered bowls on folded paper napkins.

ZONI

4 Servings

This rice cake soup is a New Year Festival dish and it is said that traditionally only wakamizu, 'young water' drawn at break of dawn on New Year's Day, is fit for this speciality, but practice has proved that ordinary water is perfectly adequate, given the other ingredients and the necessary skill in preparation. What is essential, however, is to observe the rules of presentation. Taro, spinach, carrots, etc., must be cut as described, to conform to tradition. If these vegetables are chopped up any old how, they will make some sort of a soup but it will not deserve the dignity of being called Zoni.

180 grs (6 oz or ¾ cup) raw breast of chicken
1 teaspoon cornflour
large piece kamaboko (fish paste)
1 fairly thick carrot
2–3 peeled taro roots
1 litre (2 pints or 4 cups) dashi (p 21)
shoyu
salt
60 grs (2 oz) spinach
lemon peel
8 o-mochi (glutinous rice cakes)

Cut chicken into 8 uniform pieces, flatten slightly, dip in cornflour, drop into boiling water, reduce heat and leave to simmer, so gently that the movement of water is barely perceptible, until done.

Cut kamaboko into 8 cubes.

Cut carrot into 8 slices, then with a special cutter stamp out into cherry blossom shapes. (These cutters are cheap and available from Japanese shops.) Cut taro lengthwise into 12 slices.

Boil carrot and taro in just enough dashi to cover, until soft. Season with shoyu and salt to taste.

Cook spinach for 2 minutes in salted boiling water, drain, cut into 2½ cm (1 inch) lengths. Cut lemon peel into 4 thin 'leaves', making sure all pith is shaved off.

Heat o-mochi rice cakes under the grill, without allowing them to colour.

Bring dashi to the boil, season with 1 teaspoon shoyu and a pinch of salt.

Into each bowl put 2 o-mochi cakes, 2 slices of chicken, 2 cubes of kamaboko fish paste, divide the vegetables equally, fill up the bowls with piping hot dashi, float a lemon peel 'leaf' on top, cover with lid, and serve.

SAJOER

This is an Indonesian soup which may form part of the rijstafel menu. It can be served in individual bowls or spooned over boiled rice. It is substantial enough to be a meal in itself.

8 Servings

- 3 onions
- 2 cloves garlic
- 1 teaspoon fresh ginger
- 1 teaspoon cumin seed
- 1 teaspoon coriander
- ½ teaspoon chilli powder
- 1 bay leaf
- 1 dried lemon leaf
- 2 teaspoons salt
- 3 tablespoons peanut oil
- 1½ litres (3 pints or 6 cups) coconut milk (see p 151)
- 1 carrot
- 120 grs (4 oz or ⅓ cup) runner beans
- 180 grs (6 oz or ½ cup) cabbage or Brussels sprouts
- 120 grs (4 oz or ½ cup) shelled peas
- small cauliflower
- 30 grs (1 oz or 2 tablespoons) lean beef
- 1 teaspoon grated lemon rind
- 1 sweet pepper
- 1 teaspoon paprika
- pinch brown sugar
- 240 grs (8 oz or 1½ cups) peeled prawns
- 3–4 tablespoons grated coconut

Chop 2 onions, garlic and ginger and blend in a liquidiser or pound in a mortar with cumin, coriander, chilli, bayleaf, lemon leaf and a teaspoon salt until all these ingredients are reduced to a smooth paste. Cook it for 3 minutes in 2 tablespoons hot oil, stirring constantly. Dilute with coconut milk, blend well and gently bring to the boil. Shred carrot, beans and cabbage (the cabbage can be any kind except Savoy or spring greens). Divide cauliflower into flowerets. Mince the beef. Seed and shred pepper. Add carrot, beans, cabbage, peas, cauliflower, beef, lemon rind and pepper. Season with salt and paprika, sprinkle with sugar. Cook over low heat for 15–20 minutes and make sure you have enough coconut milk to prevent drying out.

Slice the third onion finely and fry in remaining oil until very crisp. Transfer Sajoer into a serving bowl, garnish with prawns, fried onion and grated coconut and serve.

Accompaniments to Soups

MEAT PIROZHKI

6 Servings

yeast dough (p 153)
beef filling (see blinchiki p 136)
1 beaten egg for glazing
½ teaspoon salt

Roll out the dough to a thickness of ¾ cm (¼ inch) and cut into circles. Put a spoonful of filling on each circle of dough, fold over into semi-circles and pinch edges together.

Pre-heat oven to 175°C (350°F Gas Regulo 3).

Whisk egg with salt and use the mixture for brushing pirozhki.

Bake for 25–30 minutes, until pirozhki are golden. Puff pastry (p. 153) can be used instead of yeast dough. The procedure is the same except that all puff pastry preparations should be put in a refrigerator until ready to bake and should be baked in a very hot oven 230°C (450°F Gas Regulo 7).

Excellent with borsch. Serve on side plate, with butter.

CABBAGE PIROZHKI

These are great favourites. They are particularly delicious. Excellent with Russian borsch, served on the side plate and eaten instead of bread.

6 Servings

puff pastry (p 153)
240 grs (8 oz or ⅔ cup) shredded white cabbage
salt
1 small chopped onion
2 tablespoons butter
2 hard-boiled eggs
pepper
1 beaten egg for gloss

Prepare puff pastry and keep cold. Sprinkle cabbage with teaspoon salt and leave to stand for 20 minutes. Put in a collander, scald with boiling water and drain.

Fry onion in butter until soft and transparent. Squeeze surplus water out of cabbage and add to onion. Fry gently, without allowing it to brown, until soft. Remove from heat and leave until cold.

Chop the hard-boiled eggs, add to cabbage, check for salt, season with pepper.

Roll out pastry, fill pirozhki, brush with beaten egg and bake as described in oven pre-heated to 230°C (450°F or Gas Regulo 7).

RICE AND EGG PIROZHKI

6 Servings

- dough or puff pastry (p 153)
- 180 grs (6 oz or 7/8 cup) rice
- 60 grs (2 oz or 4 tablespoons) butter
- 2–3 chopped hard-boiled eggs
- 30 grs (1 oz or 3 tablespoons) chopped spring onions
- 1 tablespoon chopped parsley
- salt and pepper
- 1 beaten egg

Have the dough or pastry ready.

Boil rice in lightly salted water until done. Drain thoroughly, add half the butter and chopped eggs and mix. Heat remaining butter and fry spring onions and parsley to soften. Add to rice, season to taste with salt and pepper, remove from heat and cool the filling.

Roll out pastry, complete pirozhki as described in earlier recipes, brush with egg beaten with a pinch of salt and bake.

BUCKWHEAT AND EGG PIROZHKI

Follow recipe for Rice And Egg Pirozhki substituting cooked buckwheat (see kasha p. 150) for rice.

SALMON PIROZHKI

6 Servings

- yeast dough or puff pastry (p 153)
- 240 grs (8 oz) fresh salmon
- court-bouillon (p 20)
- 1 finely chopped onion
- 3 tablespoons butter
- 3 tablespoons cooked rice
- salt and pepper
- 1/4 teaspoon nutmeg
- 2 eggs
- fried parsley for garnish (p 148)

Prepare dough or pastry of your choice.

To make filling, poach salmon in court-bouillon until just tender. Do not overcook. Remove fish, skin, bone and flake.

Fry onion in butter until soft, without browning. Add salmon, fry together for 2 minutes. Add rice, season to taste with salt, pepper and nutmeg. Remove from heat. Add 1 lightly beaten egg, stir and allow the filling to cool.

Roll out and fill pirozhki. Use the second egg, beaten with a pinch of salt, to brush the pirozhki to give them a gloss.

Bake as described in oven pre-heated to 230°C (450°F or Gas Regulo 7), garnish with fried parsley and serve with ukha (pp. 64–65).

POTATO AND KASHA PIROZHKI

Pirozhki are patties, with various fillings, which make excellent accompaniments to borsch and other soups. They are served on the side, instead of bread. Among the popular fillings are: fish, liver, meat, mushroom, carrot, cabbage and hard-boiled egg, or spring onions and hard-boiled egg, and, of course, buckwheat – or kasha. The filling can be enclosed in puff pastry, yeast dough or potato pastry, as in the recipe which follows.

6–8 Servings

Kasha (p 150), using half quantity
4 tablespoons butter or oil
2 large chopped onions
salt and pepper
1 kg (2 lbs or 4 cups) hot mashed potato
2 eggs
self-raising flour
1 beaten egg

Prepare the kasha as described. Heat half the butter and fry the onion until soft, but do not brown. Add to kasha, season to taste with salt and pepper and stir well.

Mash the hot potato with remaining butter, add eggs, season and, adding flour as required, make a pliable dough. Roll out on a lightly floured board to a thickness of ¾ cm (¼ inch) and cut into circles with a round pastry cutter.

Put a spoonful of kasha filling on each circle, fold over into crescent shapes and pinch the edges securely. Add a pinch of salt to the beaten egg and brush the pirozhki with it to give them an attractive gloss. Pre-heat oven to 190°C (375°F or Gas Regulo 4). Bake for 20–25 minutes.

MUSHROOM PIROZHKI

6 Servings

500 grs (1 lb or 7 cups) fresh sliced mushrooms
½ teaspoon salt
¼ teaspoon pepper
3 tablespoons chopped spring onions
1 tablespoon dill or parsley
60 grs (2 oz or 4 tablespoons) butter
3 tablespoons sour cream
puff pastry (p 153)
1 egg

Put the mushrooms in a saucepan, sprinkle with salt, pepper, spring onions and dill. Stir and sweat them over low heat for a few minutes. As soon as the mushrooms yield up their juices, add butter and sour cream. Simmer gently for 10 minutes. Remove and chill before using the filling.

Roll out and cut out pastry, fill and shape pirozhki as described (p. 133). Beat egg with a pinch of salt, paint the pirozhki with a mixture to give them a lovely gloss and place in refrigerator until ready to bake.

Heat oven to 230°C (450°F or Gas Regulo 7). Bake as described and serve with consommé.

BLINCHIKI

Blinchiki is the Russian diminutive of blini – pancakes. These rolled pancakes are served as an accompaniment to clear soups. The filling for blinchiki can be of infinite variety. They are delicious with minced chicken and game leftovers, chicken livers, rice and mushrooms, salmon, veal and ham, chopped hard-boiled eggs and spring onions, lobster, prawns or crayfish, etc.

4 Servings

For batter:

120 grs (4 oz or 1 cup) self-raising flour
pinch salt
1 teaspoon sugar
1 lightly beaten egg
2½ dcl (½ pint or 1 cup) milk
butter

For filling:

1 small finely chopped onion
240 grs (8 oz or 1 cup) fresh minced beef
2 tablespoons chopped mushrooms
1–2 chopped hard-boiled eggs
4 tablespoons stock or water
salt and pepper
½ tablespoon chopped dill or parsley
a little white of egg for sealing pancake rolls

Combine flour, salt and sugar, stir in egg and gradually blend in milk. Mix well and leave for 25–30 minutes. Heat a frying pan, brush with a little butter, pour a small ladleful of batter into the pan and tilt it to spread the batter evenly over the bottom. Do not pour in more than 2½ tablespoons at a time. If you put in too much, pour it off. Fry on one side only. As soon as one side is done, turn the pancake out on to a wooden board and keep warm. Brush the pan with butter again and proceed to fry the rest of the pancakes.

Heat 2 tablespoons butter and fry onion until soft. Add beef and brown. Add mushroom, cook together for 5 minutes, stirring all the time to prevent sticking and adding more butter if necessary.

Add eggs, stock, seasoning and dill. Cook, stirring for 1–2 minutes, remove from heat.

Place the pancakes fried side up, put a spoonful of filling at one edge, fold it over, tuck in sides and roll the pancakes. Brush the edge of the outer flap with egg white to prevent unrolling.

Before serving, fry blinchiki in butter to brown lightly, drain on absorbent kitchen paper and serve with a light consommé.

Alternatively, for a posher presentation, you can dip the pancake rolls in lightly beaten egg, coat with fine sieved breadcrumbs, then fry in butter.

BLINCHIKI WITH PRAWNS

4 Servings

- Pancake batter (p 136)
- 2 lightly beaten eggs
- salt and pepper
- 2 tablespoons butter
- 240 grs (8 oz or 1 cup) peeled cooked prawns
- 30 grs (1 oz or 4 tablespoons) grated breadcrumbs
- 2 tablespoons cream
- ¼ teaspoon nutmeg
- fried parsley (p 148)

Prepare batter as described. Season beaten egg with salt and pepper. Melt butter and gently scramble the eggs. As soon as the egg mixture begins to set, add prawns, breadcrumbs, cream and nutmeg. Finish cooking, stirring until the eggs set. Remove from heat and cool. Fry, fill and fry pancake rolls as described. Garnish with fried parsley and serve with ukha (pp. 64–65).

BLINCHATY PIROG

This is rather a *de luxe* pancake pie which in a Russian menu is classed as an accompaniment to clear soups, but is substantial and interesting enough to be served as an independent course. Served with a good consommé it would certainly require only a light dessert, or simply fruit, to make a complete meal.

The recipe looks more elaborate than it is. It is possible to do most of the preparation of this rewarding dish well in advance, so that all you will have to do would be to pre-heat the oven and bake the pie.

6 Servings

- pancake batter (p 136)
- butter
- beef filling (see blinchiki p 136)
- 2½ dcl (½ pint or 1 cup) Béchamel sauce (p 22)
- Cream cheese filling (p 140)
- parsley

Fry the pancakes on both sides. Butter a deep soufflé dish to match the pancakes in diameter. Line the bottom with a pancake. Put a layer of beef filling and spread some Béchamel over it. Cover with a pancake, spread with a layer of cream cheese filling. Continue in this way, alternating beef and Béchamel filling with cream cheese, until all is used up. Finish off with a pancake, scatter a few dabs of butter on top and bake in a hot oven, pre-heated to 230°C (450°F Gas Regulo 7), long enough to heat through and brown the top. Turn out on to a heated serving dish, decorate with parsley. To serve cut into wedges, as you would a layer cake.

SALMON COULIBIAC

8–10 Servings

For coulibiac dough:

- 500 gr (1 lb or 4 cups) sifted flour
- 25 gr ($\frac{3}{4}$ oz or $1\frac{1}{2}$ cakes) baker's yeast
- 4 eggs
- 1 teaspoon sugar
- pinch salt
- $1\frac{1}{2}$ dcl (1 gill or $\frac{1}{2}$ cup) warm milk
- 185 gr (6 oz or $\frac{3}{4}$ cup) softened butter

Filling:

- 750 gr ($1\frac{1}{2}$ lb) fresh salmon
- butter
- 250 gr ($\frac{1}{2}$ lb or $1\frac{1}{8}$ cups) rice (or buckwheat)
- stock (optional)
- 3–4 chopped hard-boiled eggs
- 125 gr (4 oz or 2 cups) sliced mushrooms
- 1 chopped onion
- 1 tablespoon chopped parsley
- 4 tablespoons madeira
- salt and pepper
- pinch nutmeg
- 1 tablespoon chopped chives
- sieved breadcrumbs

Firstly, prepare the coulibiac dough. To make leaven, put a quarter of the flour in a circle on the table, put the yeast in the middle, dilute with a little water, mix, moistening from time to time, to keep the dough on the soft side. Roll into a ball, make a crossways incision in the top, cover and leave in a warm place for the leaven to ferment and double its volume. Put the rest of the flour in a circle on the table, put eggs and 2 tablespoons of warm water in the middle, moisten the dough with milk and knead it. Add sugar and salt dissolved in a teaspoon of water and incorporate the softened butter. Mix well, spread the dough on the table, pour the leaven into the middle, blend it in, put the dough in a bowl, cover with a clean cloth and leave in a warm place to rise – this fermentation process takes 5 to 6 hours. When it has risen, beat the dough and from then on keep in a cool place until ready to roll out.

Cut the salmon into small pieces and fry lightly in butter, just to stiffen them. Remove and allow to cool.

Cook the rice in water (or stock). Fry the mushrooms and onion lightly in butter, add parsley, madeira, salt, pepper, nutmeg and chives, then add salmon and simmer for a few minutes. Remove from heat.

Using two-thirds of the dough, roll out the bottom sheet, which has to be thicker than the top covering. Put on a lightly greased baking sheet. Spread the filling, avoiding the edges, in layers: first half the rice. Then arrange the salmon, scatter mushrooms and their juices over it, follow with a layer of hard-boiled eggs and finally another layer of rice. Dot with tiny pieces of butter. Roll out the rest of the dough, cover the filling carefully with it. Moisten the edges slightly to make the dough stick together and draw up the edges of the lower sheet of pastry, so that they cover the edge of the upper sheet. Cut a slit in the top to enable steam to escape, brush the top with melted butter, sprinkle with breadcrumbs, and bake in a moderately hot oven 240°C (460°F or Gas Regulo 5) for 1 hour. Remove from oven, pour 3–4 tablespoons melted butter into the 'chimney hole' in the centre and serve.

TAMARA'S GEORGIAN MEAT COULIBIAC

Coulibiacs and pies are to a Russian birthday party what birthday cakes are elsewhere in the world. Birthday invitations, in fact, ask people not to lunch or dinner but to a coulibiac or pirog, which are always served with soup.

For people who have birthdays during Lent, a fish coulibiac with ukha used to be served, which was no hardship at all.

Meat coulibiacs are served with a clear consommé.

6–8 Servings

- Dough for coulibiac (*see* salmon coulibiac, p 138)
- 500–750 grs (1–1½ lbs) steak
- butter
- 1 bunch chopped spring onions
- 250 grs (½ lb or 3½ cups) sliced mushrooms
- 30 grs (1 oz or ¾ cup) chopped parsley
- salt and pepper
- stock
- sieved breadcrumbs

Prepare the coulibiac dough as described.

Cut the steak into strips, fry in 3 teaspoons butter. When brown on all sides, add spring onions, mushrooms, and parsley. Mix, and cook together for 5 minutes. Season with salt and pepper, and moisten with 2 or 3 tablespoons stock.

Using two-thirds of the dough, roll out the bottom sheet, which has to be thicker than the top covering. Put on a lightly greased baking sheet. Spread the filling, avoiding the edges. Dot with tiny pieces of butter. Roll out the rest of the dough, cover the filling carefully with it. Moisten the edges slightly to make the dough stick together, and draw up the edges of the lower sheet of pastry, so that they cover the edge of the upper sheet. Cut a slit in the top to enable steam to escape, brush the top with melted butter, sprinkle with breadcrumbs, and bake in a moderately hot oven 205°C (400°F or Gas Regulo 5) for 1 hour. Remove from oven, pour 3 to 4 tablespoons melted butter into the 'chimney hole' in the centre, and serve.

CREAM CHEESE TARTLETS TO SERVE WITH SOUP

These tartlets are traditionally served with borsch, shchi, spinach soup, sorrel soup, etc.

pastry for tartlets (p 153)
½ kg (1 lb or 2 cups) cream cheese
2–3 tablespoons sour cream
pinch salt and pepper
½ tablespoon sugar
2 eggs
1 tablespoon butter

Prepare pastry and leave. Mix cream cheese with sour cream, season with salt and pepper, add sugar and eggs and mix well.

Roll out pastry and fill individual oval or round tartlet tins. Spoon filling into tartlets, dot each with a dab of butter. Bake for 20–25 minutes in oven preheated to 190°C (375°F or Gas Regulo 4).

BUCKWHEAT CROÛTONS

All buckwheat preparations, croûtons, pirozhki and just plain kasha are traditional accompaniments to borsch, light clear soups and shchi. And very good they are, too!

6 Servings

180 grs (6 oz or 1 cup) cooked buckwheat (*see* kasha p 150)
3–4 tablespoons butter
salt and pepper

Place the cooked buckwheat in a large oblong dish, slightly moistened with water. Press down to a thickness of 1¼ cm (½ inch), cover with another dish rinsed out with cold water and allow to cool between the two dishes with a light weight on top. Trim off any rough edges, cut into neat slices and fry in sizzling butter. Brown on both sides turning carefully. Drain on absorbent paper and serve.

STUFFED EGGS

- 6 eggs
- 60 grs (2 oz or 4 tablespoons) butter
- 1 teaspoon salt
- ¼ teaspoon pepper
- 2 tablespoons chopped parsley
- 2 tablespoons toasted bread-crumbs
- 1 raw egg

Boil the eggs for 7 to 8 minutes, plunge in cold water, then cut lengthwise with a sharp knife taking care not to break up the shells. Take out the eggs and chop up finely. Melt 3 tablespoons butter in a saucepan, put in eggs for a few seconds, remove from heat, add salt, pepper, parsley, breadcrumbs and egg. Blend well, fill the shells with the mixture, sprinkle with breadcrumbs, put a piece of butter on each and put in the oven or under a grill to brown. Serve with Spinach or Sorrel Soup on separate plates, garnished with fried parsley (p. 148).

Soup Garnishes

CHEESE QUENELLES

120 grs (4 oz or 1 cup) cheese (Cheddar, Dutch or Parmesan)
1 tablespoon butter
2 eggs
60 grs (2 oz) bread soaked in 6 tablespoons milk
1 tablespoon sour cream
30 grs (1 oz) toasted breadcrumbs

Grate the cheese, add butter, pound together into a smooth mixture, add eggs, bread, previously soaked in milk, and sour cream. Mix well, roll into walnut-sized balls, dip in toasted breadcrumbs and drop into stock. As soon as they float up to the surface, they are ready to be served.

CHICKEN QUENELLES

Remove flesh from chicken and use bones for stock. Cut up the flesh and mince it. Proceed as described in recipe for Cheese Quenelles.

KIDNEY QUENELLES

Follow recipe for Veal Quenelles (p. 30) but substitute 2 calf's kidneys for veal. Put the kidneys into boiling water, bring up to the boil, remove, rinse well, take off the skins and membranes, then proceed as with Veal Quenelles.

LIVER BALLS FOR SOUP

30 grs (1 oz or $\frac{7}{8}$ cup) freshly grated breadcrumbs
4–5 tablespoons stock
120 grs (4 oz or $\frac{1}{2}$ cup) minced chicken livers
$\frac{1}{2}$ teaspoon grated onion
salt and pepper
1 beaten egg

Mix breadcrumbs with stock, simmer over low heat stirring to amalgamate. Remove from heat, add liver, onion and seasoning. Bind with egg, shape into balls and cook in soup for 10–12 minutes.

CROÛTONS

To make croûtons cut crustless slices of bread into cubes or into various shapes, triangles, hearts, half-moons, lozenges – or stamp them out with small pastry cutters – and fry in butter or oil until golden all over. Croûtons can also be dried in the oven.

To make potato croûtons, dice raw potato, fry as above and drain on absorbent kitchen paper.

RAVIOLI

375 grs (12 oz or 3 cups) flour
pinch salt
2 eggs
30 grs (1 oz or 2 tablespoons) softened butter
scant 240 ml ($\frac{1}{2}$ pint or 1 cup) warm water

To make ravioli paste sift flour and salt on to a pastry board, make a well in the middle, break the eggs into it, fold the flour into them as for noodle paste (p. 154). Add butter, knead and little by little incorporate enough water to make a smooth stiff dough. Cover with a floured cloth and leave to stand for 10 minutes. Divide into 2 or 3 parts, depending on the size of your pastry board, roll out on a floured board until very thin.

Spread the rolled out paper-thin sheets of paste on a cloth and cover with another cloth, to prevent drying and preserve elasticity.

For filling, put a teaspoon of stuffing on one sheet of paste, allowing about $3\frac{3}{4}$ cm ($1\frac{1}{2}$ inches) intervals between the little mounds of filling. Trace demarcation lines between the spoonfuls of filling with a pastry brush dipped in beaten egg. Cover with a second sheet of paste, then proceed to cut out your ravioli.

The cutting can be done either by running a pastry wheel along the traced out lines, which will give you little square pillow shapes, or by pressing out with a round pastry cutter, not more than $3\frac{3}{4}$ cm ($1\frac{1}{2}$ inches) in diameter. Keep the cut out ravioli on a lightly floured board; do not overlap or stack them in layers. Cover with a floured cloth until ready to use. Ravioli can be made in advance and kept in a refrigerator between sheets of waxed paper. Boil them as you would any pasta, in plenty of salted boiling water.

Carefully remove from pan with a perforated spoon, transfer to a heated soup tureen, pour on boiling consommé and serve with grated Parmesan cheese.

SOUP NUTS

These little pellets of dough, baked or deep fried, look like nuts. The Yiddish name for them is mandeln, which means almonds.

- 2 eggs
- 2 tablespoons oil
- 180 gr (6 oz or 1½ cups) sifted flour
- pinch salt
- pinch baking powder
- fat for deep frying, if the nuts are to be fried

Beat eggs with oil, add flour, salt and baking powder and mix into a soft dough. Chill for 30 minutes. With your hands roll portions of dough into thin little sausages, no more than 1¼ cm (½ inch) thick. Cut into 1¼ cm (½ inch) pieces. Then either bake or deep fry. To bake, put on a greased baking sheet and cook in the oven pre-heated to 190°C (375°F or Gas Regulo 4), shaking from time to time until the nuts are uniformly golden brown.

To deep fry, heat the fat, drop the pellets of dough into it, until they puff up and turn golden brown, drain. Whether you bake or fry the soup nuts, serve them piping hot.

VARENIKI WITH CHERRIES

6–8 Servings

- Noodle paste (p 154)
- 1 kg (2 lb) cherries
- 180 grs (6 oz or ¾ cup) sugar

Prepare dough as described. Stone the cherries, preserving all the juice, add sugar and leave for 3–4 hours.

Crush 5–6 cherry stones into fine powder, add to cherries and put them into a saucepan with 2½ dcl (½ pint or 1 cup) water. Bring to the boil, cook for 2 minutes and strain, keeping all the liquid. Roll out the dough, cut, fill vareniki with 2–3 cherries each and boil for 10 minutes. These make excellent garnish for clear borsch (p. 89). To use up leftover vareniki as a dessert, boil them in plain water.

Remove with a perforated spoon, put in a heated serving dish and keep warm.

Boil down the strained juice left from cooking the cherries until it thickens and becomes syrupy.

Serve this sauce and sour cream with vareniki.

KREPLACH

Kreplach are a famous Jewish speciality. They are triangular or square, ravioli-like pasta pockets with various fillings. They can be boiled in water, drained and served on their own or in soup. Kreplach are traditionally served at various Jewish festivals. To serve with soup, cook the kreplach in boiling salted water for 12 to 15 minutes, or until they float to the surface, drain and add to soup.

Noodle paste (p 154)
½ kg (1 lb or 2 cups) minced cooked meat
1 tablespoon finely grated onion
1 tablespoon chopped parsley
salt and pepper to taste
pinch powdered ginger
1–2 eggs, depending on size

Prepare noodle paste as described.

Combine meat (beef, veal, beef sausage meat, chicken), onion, parsley, salt, pepper and ginger. Mix well, stir in eggs to bind the mixture.

Put the noodle paste on a lightly floured board, roll out thinly, cut into squares not bigger than 5 cm (2 inches).

Put a teaspoon of the filling in the middle of each square, fold into a triangle, press to enclose the filling, then bring the two corners together and press hard to seal the edges. Leave on a floured board for an hour or so to dry.

Cook in boiling salted water, drain by removing them carefully with a perforated spoon and use as required.

FARFEL

Using noodle paste (p. 154), knead, roll into a ball and leave for 45 minutes. Grate on a coarse grater, leave on a cloth or board to dry. Drop into strained boiling broth and cook in the same way as noodles.

MEAT BALLS FOR SOUP

180 gr (6 oz or ¾ cup) raw minced beef
1½ teaspoons finely grated onion
1 teaspoon finely chopped parsley
pinch grated lemon rind
salt and pepper to taste
pinch nutmeg
1 beaten egg

Combine all ingredients, mix well, roll into small balls and boil them in strained broth for 15 minutes.

MATZO MEAT DUMPLINGS FOR SOUP

180 gr (6 oz or 1½ cups) matzo meat

160 ml ($5\frac{1}{2}$ oz or $\frac{2}{3}$ cup) water
salt and pepper
pinch grated nutmeg
3 eggs
6 tablespoons oil

Mix matzo meat with water, season to taste with salt, pepper and nutmeg.

Beat the eggs and whisk them into the batter. Blend in oil. Chill the batter for 4 hours.

Taking a little mixture at a time, shape into balls or quenelles. To cook, drop the dumplings into strained boiling broth a few at a time, allowing boiling to be re-established again before adding more dumplings, simmer for 35–40 minutes.

ALMOND DUMPLINGS FOR CHICKEN SOUP

2 eggs
90 gr (3 oz or 1 cup) ground almonds
pinch salt
$\frac{1}{2}$ teaspoon grated lemon rind
fat for deep frying

Separate the eggs and mix the yolks with almonds. Add salt and lemon rind.

Whisk the egg whites until very stiff and fold into the almond mixture.

Heat fat. Using a coffee spoon, take a little of the mixture at a time, drop into fat, cook as described in recipe for soup nuts (p. 145). Drain well and serve at once while the dumplings are still crisp.

POTATO DUMPLINGS

3 medium-sized potatoes
750 ml ($1\frac{1}{2}$ pints or 3 cups) water
1 teaspoon salt
1 tablespoon butter
2 tablespoons flour
2 raw yolks
2 stiffly beaten whites of egg

Peel, slice and boil the potatoes in water. After they come to the boil, add salt and continue to simmer for 15 to 20 minutes. Strain and rub through a sieve while still hot. Add butter, flour and the yolks. Blend well together, add beaten whites, mix thoroughly. 10 minutes before serving, drop the dumplings into boiling stock, or salted water. Using a teaspoon, dip the spoon into a cup of cold water, scoop up half a teaspoonful of the mixture at a time and quickly shake it off into the stock. Continue until all the mixture is used up. Cook the dumplings on a low heat. As soon as they float up to the surface – they are done.

FRIED PARSLEY

30–60 grs (1–2 oz) parsley | 1 tablespoon melted butter

Wash the parsley, cut off the long stalks, dip lightly in melted butter and put in a hot oven to dry off. Be careful not to burn.

Alternative method: Heat a large cup of olive oil until it begins to smoke. Trim, wash and dry the parsley on a cloth, drop into sizzling oil for two minutes, stir, take out with a perforated spoon, drain on a piece of kitchen paper, sprinkle with salt and use for garnishing pirozhki, etc.

Auxiliary Recipes: Forcemeats, Dips, Fillings, etc.

SPINACH AND CHICKEN FILLING FOR RAVIOLI

250 grs (8 oz or 1 cup) cooked spinach pureé
250 grs (8 oz or 1 cup) cooked finely chopped or minced chicken
60 grs (2 oz or ½ cup) grated breadcrumbs
60 grs (2 oz or ½ cup) grated Parmesan cheese
½ clove pounded garlic (optional)
1 tablespoon finely chopped parsley
salt
freshly ground black pepper
2 beaten eggs

Combine all the ingredients, bind with eggs, mix well, check seasoning and use the filling as described.

VEAL FILLING FOR RAVIOLI

250 grs (8 oz or 1 cup) diced lean veal
60 grs (2 oz or 4 tablespoons) butter
stock or water with stock cube
1 dcl (1 gill or ½ cup) red wine
1 slice crustless bread
milk
125 grs (4 oz or ½ cup) cooked drained spinach
60 grs (2 oz or ½ cup) grated Parmesan cheese
2 tablespoons finely chopped onion
salt
freshly ground black pepper
2 beaten eggs

Fry the veal in butter to brown on all sides, add enough stock just to cover the bottom of the pan and simmer for 15 minutes. Moisten with wine and cook until tender. Pour enough milk over the bread to soak it, then squeeze out surplus milk.

Pass the veal, bread and spinach through a mincer. Add cheese, and onion, season with salt and pepper to taste, blend in eggs to bind and mix thoroughly.

KASHA (BAKED BUCKWHEAT)

500 gr (1 lb or 2⅔ cups) buckwheat
1 teaspoon salt
60 gr (2 oz or 4 tablespoons) butter
boiling water

Sort the buckwheat and pick out any black grains. Roast it in an ungreased frying pan, stirring and taking care not to burn, until pale golden. Put in an ovenproof dish, season with salt, stir in butter and pour in enough boiling water to cover. Bake in a slow oven, 135°C (275°F or Gas Regulo 2) for 2½ to 3 hours.

HAWAYIJ

This is one of a series of Yemeni bread dips.

These blends of spices, reminiscent of the Indian garam-masala below, are splendid for giving flavour to a simple meal. The Yemenites further claim that their immunity to coronary diseases, as well as to high blood pressure and the digestive troubles which afflict the Western world, is due to their use of these spice dips from time immemorial to the present day.

The Sabra cooks have adopted all these dips as seasoning for many dishes.

2 tablespoons black pepper
1 teaspoon saffron
1 tablespoon caraway seeds
1 teaspoon cardamom
2 teaspoons turmeric

Grind all ingredients, blend well. Transfer to a jar with a tightly fitting lid and store until required.

BALACHAUNG

24 dried prawns
1 knob green ginger
1–2 teaspoons ground chilli
6 tablespoons tamarind or lime juice
¼ pint ghee or clarified butter (see p 23)
2 fresh (or dry) curry leaves (optional)

Rinse the prawns and pat dry on a cloth. Mince or chop ginger finely. Pound prawns in a mortar, sprinkle with ginger, chillies and tamarind juice and mix.

Heat the butter and fry the curry leaves for 1–2 minutes. Add prawn mixture, fry stirring for 10–12 minutes.

GARAM-MASALA

60 grs (2 oz or ½ cup) coriander seeds

60 grs (2 oz or ½ cup) black peppercorns
45 grs (1½ oz or 6 tablespoons) caraway seeds
15 grs (½ oz or 6 teaspoons) cloves
20 peeled cardamon seeds
15 grs (½ oz or 2 tablespoons) ground cinnamon

Mix all ingredients and grind. Store in a jar with a well-fitting lid.

COCONUT MILK

Fresh or desiccated coconut can yield both cream and milk and this can be used for enriching many preparations. It lends a velvety smoothness and mellowness to soups and is a lighter liaison than yolks of egg.

1 fresh coconut
120 ml (4 oz or ½ – 1 cup) boiling water

To make coconut cream:

Have the greengrocer saw the coconut in half, pour out the liquid. (The natural and drinkable liquid inside the coconut is *not* coconut milk.) Extract the flesh by scraping it out. Pour boiling water over it and let it stand for 20 minutes. Squeeze out in a muslin bag or pass through a fine strainer. (An Indian restaurateur advocates the use of a potato presser for extracting coconut milk.) This first pressing produces coconut cream, which after several hours' refrigeration acquires the density of double cream.

To make coconut milk:

Put the husks of the coconut which has been pressed to extract cream into a pan, add the same amount of water as for the first pressing, bring to the boil and press out again. Both coconut cream and milk can be made in a liquidiser. Observe the indicated proportions, and blend a couple of tablespoonfuls of grated or shredded coconut and water at a time. Then squeeze through a muslin bag as described.

If fresh coconut is not available good quality desiccated coconut may be used.

Dough and Pastry used for Soup Accompaniments

YEAST DOUGH FOR PIROZHKI

30 grs (1 oz or 2 cakes) fresh yeast
1 tablespoon sugar
480 ml (16 oz or 2 cups) lukewarm milk
480 grs (1 lb or 4 cups) flour
3 lightly beaten eggs
120 grs (4 oz or ½ cup) melted butter
small pinch salt

Mix yeast with sugar and dissolve with 120 ml (4 oz or ½ cup) milk.

Sift flour into a mixing bowl, add diluted yeast and stir well. Cover with a cloth and leave to rise for 30 minutes. Beat in eggs, then butter and add the rest of the milk. Sprinkle in salt and knead. When the dough becomes elastic, leave to rise again until it doubles its bulk, when it will be ready for rolling out.

Mix flour with a pinch of salt, cut in fat with a knife and add enough iced water to bind the pastry, sprinkling the water in a tablespoonful at a time, and blending it in evenly. Roll out and proceed as indicated in individual recipes.

PASTRY FOR TARTLETS

4 Servings
125 grs (4 oz or 1 cup) flour
salt
125 grs (4 oz or 8 tablespoons) butter
iced water

Mix flour with a pinch of salt, cut in fat with a knife and add enough iced water to bind the pastry, sprinkling the water in a tablespoonful at a time, and blending it in evenly. Roll out and proceed as indicated in individual recipes.

QUICK PUFF PASTRY

125 gr (4 oz or ½ cup) butter or margarine
250 gr (8 oz or 2 cups) flour
½ teaspoon salt
4 raw yolks
7 tablespoons cold water
1 tablespoon lemon juice

Using a palette knife, cut the fat into the flour, add salt, continue to mix, incorporate yolks, water and lemon juice, work with the knife until the paste is smooth, then put on a lightly floured board. Roll out to a thickness of ¾ cm (¼ inch), fold and leave to rest for 10 minutes. Repeat the rolling and folding process 3 times.

NOODLE PASTE

240 grs (8 oz or 2 cups) flour
7½ grs (¼ oz or 1½ teaspoons) salt
2 whole eggs, lightly beaten
2 yolks
cold water

Sift the flour and salt, add eggs and yolks and enough cold water to make a firm paste. Roll out, fold twice, allow to cool for an hour before using.

GLOSSARY

ABALONE – A molusc used in many Chinese dishes. Excellent in soups. Don't hold its appearance against it when you get it out of a tin. It is a clever molusc. Not only does it enrich Chinese and Japanese soups, but the shell which is its dress provides mother of pearl.

AJI-NO-MOTO – Japanese seasoning powder, known as Ve-Tsin in Chinese cookery.

ALLSPICE – Dried unripe berry of an evergreen tree, native of West Indies and Central America. Used in cooking for imparting fragrance.

BALACHAUNG – A condiment which crops up again and again under variations of the name in many Eastern countries. See recipe (p. 150).

BASIL – Herb belonging to mint family, used for its spicy flavour. Italian pesto would be unthinkable without it.

BEAN CURD (TOFU) – A unique Chinese invention, full of proteins and calcium, very cheap and absolutely delicious. One of the ingredients of Hot and Sour Pork.

BISQUE – French name originally for game soups. From 19th century applied mainly to thick shellfish soups.

BLANCHING – Scalding various ingredients with boiling water or boiling them for 1–2 minutes, then rinsing with cold water. The process seals colour and vitamins, makes peeling and skinning easier (almonds), gets rid of pungent tastes (kidneys).

BLINCHIKI – Diminutive of the Russian word blini – pancakes. Blinchiki are usually stuffed and rolled. Served as an accompaniment to clear soups.

BOUILLON – Stock (see also Pot-au-feu p. 25).

BOUQUET-GARNI – A faggot or bunch of herbs, normally containing 3 sprigs of parsley, one sprig of thyme and one small bay leaf.

BRUNOISE – Finely shredded or diced vegetables, cooked in butter or other fat.

BUCKWHEAT – Blé noir, a variety of Saracen corn, used for making

Russian kasha.

CHIFFONADE – Vegetables, particularly lettuce and sorrel, cut into fine strips or ribbons.

CHORIZO – Hard, Spanish paprika-spiced sausage.

COULIBIAC – A Russian pie, usually served hot, made of brioche or puff pastry, with various fillings, served with soup.

COURT-BOUILLON – Aromatised liquid for cooking fish, meat, vegetables, mushrooms.

CROUTONS – Bread cut in dice or sliced, of any shape or size, fried in oil, butter or another fat, toasted under the grill or dried in the oven. Often served with purέed soups.

DASHI – Japanese stock, based on dried bonito shavings and konbu seaweed.

FUMET – Concentrated fish stock.

GARAM-MASALA – A mixture of ground spices, essential ingredient of mulligatawny soup and all curry dishes.

GHEE – Clarified butter, originally made from buffalo milk, used in Indian cookery and available in tins.

HAWAYIJ – A mixture of ground spices much used in Yemeni cooking.

JULIENNE – Food cut to match-like shreds.

KASHA – See buckwheat. Kasha is used as filling for pirozhki and for croûtons which are served with soups. It is also served on its own and with shchi. (See recipe p. 150).

KOMBU – Tangle or kelp, seaweed ingredient of dashi.

KVAS – Beverage made from rye bread. Also used for making Russian cold soups. Essential ingredient of okroshka. (See recipe p. 22).

MIREPOIX – Diced onions, carrots and celery simmered, with a sprig of thyme and a fragment of bay leaf, in butter or other fat, until tender. Added to soups to enhance flavour.

MIRIN – Japanese sweet wine, used for flavouring soups. A light sherry may be used as a substitute, although mirin is easily obtainable from Japanese shops.

PEANUT OIL – The best oil for cooking. Both 700 million Chinese and 50 million Frenchmen think so – and they should know! It can be used for cooking anything, for it imparts neither flavour nor smell. Essential in Chinese cookery.

PESTO – Italian sauce, made of fresh basil, pounded with garlic, pine nuts and Parmesan and/or Sardo cheese. Used for flavouring chicken soups with pasta, minestrone and many others.

PIROZHKI – Diminutive of the Russian word *pirog,* which means a pie. Pirozhki are small patties made of different kinds of dough or pastry and with a vast variety of fillings. Classical accompaniments to many Russian soups.

POT-AU-FEU – French method of cooking broth. Pot-au-feu provides both soup and a dish of boiled meat and vegetables. (See recipe (p. 25).

ROUX – A mixture of butter or other fats and flour, cooked together and used for thickening soups.

SAKE – Japanese rice wine used for drinking and flavouring. Available in Japanese food shops. Brandy or dry sherry may be used as substitutes.

SHAO SHING – Chinese yellow wine used for drinking and flavouring. For drinking it is served hot. Good dry sherry, which Shao Shing resembles in taste, may be used as a substitute. Shao Shing is sold in all Chinese food emporia.

SHOYU – Japanese soya sauce.

SOYA SAUCE – Most popular seasoning in Chinese cooking. Liquid made from soya beans. Excellent for bringing out flavours and enhancing textures.

TABASCO – A bottled sauce made of capsicums. Very hot and spicy. Should be used sparingly.

TAMARIND – The juice of tamarind fruit is widely used throughout the East in the way vinegar is used in the West. Available in shops specialising in Oriental produce.

TOFU – *See* bean curd.

UKHA – Russian fish soup. (See recipe pp. 64–65.)

VE-TSIN – Monosodium glutamate originally produced from seaweed, used as a flavouring in China and Japan for many centuries. There is an American product marketed under the name of 'Accent'. Many dishes do not need Ve-Tsin at all, but when it is recommended, use it sparingly. After all, it is supposed to bring out flavour, not to smother it.

WATERZOOTJE – A very solid Flemish soup. More often made of fish; can also be made of chicken.

ZONE – Japanese New Year soup.

Index